WALT WHITMAN

Allen & Co. Sc.

Walt Whitman

at the age of 53

WALT WHITMAN

A CRITICAL STUDY

BY

BASIL DE SELINCOURT

NEW YORK / RUSSELL & RUSSELL

FIRST PUBLISHED IN 1914
REISSUED, 1965, BY RUSSELL & RUSSELL
A DIVISION OF ATHENEUM PUBLISHERS, INC.
L. C. CATALOG CARD NO: 64-66391
PRINTED IN THE UNITED STATES OF AMERICA

NOTE

My aim in the following study has been to lay stress on aspects of the subject which court misunderstanding or have received relatively little attention hitherto. Whitman's communication in its initial attack is so infectious and clear that it would have been self-indulgence to expatiate upon it.

CONTENTS

I

BIOGRAPHICAL

. . . *Before all my arrogant poems the real Me stands yet untouch'd, untold,*
Withdrawn far, mocking me with mock-congratulatory signs and bows,
With peals of distant ironical laughter at every word I have written.

Every aspect of a man's character is reflected both in his life and in his work ; but some are more easily read in the one, some in the other glass. In spite of all his efforts to communicate his personality, Whitman remains in many respects so mysterious a figure that, although we are concerned here with a literary rather than a biographical estimate, we shall most readily establish an understanding with our readers by giving an outline of our hero's story and placing his typical actions, ambitions and achievements in what seems to be their natural light. He was a born poet, and his genius is not least exhibited in his recognition of the dependence of expression upon experience. This, again, makes an acquaintance with the main facts of his history important to the student of his art. Too many artists, confusing experience with experiment, look upon the world as a training-ground in which to disport themselves and become versatile and accomplished. Yet life does not yield its flavour to him who would merely taste it ; that alone is true experience to which the whole personality is pledged. Nothing more distinguishes an artist of the first from one of the second rank than his instinct for living. To what extent was this instinct Whitman's ?

There is little in his antecedents to explain the appearance of a great artist in the family. He came of a race of small yeomen farmers, and the Dutch stubbornness which he inherited from his mother might have been expected to emphasise New England's natural bent towards taciturnity. But mother and father alike, as is clear from the well-known photographs, were persons of unusual and emphatic character. The father's face expresses a capacity for thought and idealism which everyday cares have fretted into disuse and tinctured with some bitterness ; in the mother's unconscious power rides, and we see her meeting every situation, serene and adequate. Devotion to his mother was to be the dominant feature of Walt's emotional life.

BIOGRAPHICAL

Born on the 31st of May, 1819, the poet was the second of a family of nine children, the first and last of whom, both boys, were mentally defective, while another died in infancy. He was therefore in effect the eldest of a brood of six—two girls, four boys—and, inheriting all his mother's serenity, early assumed the responsibilities of guide and counsellor.

The important facts of his childhood are those which his own poems chronicle. He is indeed said to have been noticed among a crowd of Brooklyn children, and even to have been kissed, by Lafayette at the age of five. But whether this was a sign of Walter's precocity or of Lafayette's perception, history does not tell us. Perhaps a mere accident has been allowed to assume premonitory associations. The general effect we derive from the sparse narratives extant, as well as from Whitman's own memories and impressions, is that in childhood he must have been a heavy absorptive creature who might have been liable to the penalties of extreme sensitiveness but for the fact that his susceptibility was as wide as it was keen.

> There was a child went forth,

and if the impressions which the child received were so vivid that they became a part of him, they were also so various that there was little danger of any part overbalancing the whole. Words of his own were not needed to assure us that the first and greatest of them was the impression of the sea. His earliest impulse to composition came from the sight of a ship under full sail, and the idea he was afterwards to form for his poetry was that the seashore should be an invisible influence in it, a "pervading gauge and tally."

If sensitiveness and absorption are the words of his childhood, those of his adolescence are absorption and restlessness. The customs of the still rapidly developing society to which he belonged were all in favour of general intelligence and handiness. It was natural enough that Walt should see in succession the workings of a doctor's and of a lawyer's office; that he should learn printing and carpentering, should give a year or two to school teaching, and then become founder and editor of a news-sheet, printed by himself and by himself distributed among the simple inhabitants of his native Long Island. At the age of twenty he has thus intuitively arrived at the career which fits him; he is to be a recorder of life, an interpreter of ideas through the written word. Nothing remains to be decided except the scale and scope his work is to assume.

At what point he became conscious of a mission we do not know; but his early work shows that he had from the beginning a strongly developed moral purpose and felt himself in a narrower sense than we might expect vowed to the service of good causes. In his first compositions he generally contrived to exhibit the terrible end of the profligate's career, or repentance instilled by the brave words of the youth who still prays as he did by his mother's knee. Trite as they are, these pieces are readable, both for the vividness of the narrative and also because we feel behind them the sweetness and courage which they imperfectly extol. The climax in this line was a novel dedicated to the cause of Temperance, though written, if legends are to be believed, with occasional assistance from gin punch. The word morality took on larger associations with Whitman as his experience of life increased; but there is no evidence in his youth of a period in which the conventional "good" seemed counterfeit. Reaction and rebellion were to be the weapons, rather, of his maturity.

His taste in literature was in accordance with this view of him. We hear that he was an omnivorous novel-reader and "devoured everything he could get." Probably there was little enough to be got in this line in Long

Island a century ago; and the boy's favourite reading was in prose the *Arabian Nights*, in poetry the works of Scott. There could be no better indication of the essential simplicity of his character. Subjugated as he was by the largest and most indefinable aspects of Nature, already, no doubt, living unconsciously in a key dictated by his instinctive sympathy with the sky and the sea, his mind fastened upon common tangible objects and took pleasure in the genial display of things which are displayed easily and to advantage. This is a trait that must be emphasised, because our understanding of his poetry turns on the background upon which we place it, and it is difficult for the sophisticated reader to supply a background sufficiently obvious and unadorned. His simplicity was individual, but it was also racial. Whitman is not the only great American writer who at times misleads us by over-elaboration of language, tempting us to look in his words for more meaning than he intends them to convey.

What the sea was to him among the works of nature, music was among the works of man—was, or might have been.

> Ah from a little child,

he writes in *Proud Music of the Storm*,

> Thou knowest soul how to me all sounds became music·

but of true music, nevertheless, his experience was small. Speaking of his dislike for 'piano-tunes,' he concedes that he has never heard the instrument well played, and his impression of Beethoven's *Septet*, delicately appreciative as it is and worthy of a poet, reveals that he knew no other chamber-music. Perhaps it was as well that music, like literature, should be represented to him in its broader outlines. Through life he brought to it an elemental childlike impressionability and an inexhaustible child's ardour, composing many of his poems under the influence of emotions which it had engendered. But the art was represented to him in the main by opera, and whether in opera he cared more for the musical or the dramatic element it would be hard to say. He was a devoted theatre-goer, and had strong histrionic sympathies. The singer, the stage, the footlights, the whole machinery of effect, produced their effect upon him, and no artificial heightening of pageantry or expression lifted them for him too high. When Alboni, his favourite cantatrice, or some renowned tragedian, a Keen or a Booth, was in the town, he would be nightly in the pit, audience and actors affording him between them a twofold drama. Like Blake he inverted the old Greek proverb, and by "Nothing too much" meant not that nothing should but that nothing could be so.

His experience with *The Long Islander* brought him into contact with the journalistic and Bohemian life of New York, where he edited several papers and affected for a time—a short time—the dress and demeanour of a dandy. Here too, as Mr. John Burroughs tells us, being " young, in perfect bodily condition," he " sounded all experiences of life, with all their pleasures, passions and abandonments." If the phrase were from the pen of a European writer, we should know that not only the dandy but the rake also had been among Walt's affectations; and whatever its meaning it has as it stands a sufficiently distasteful sound. But what displeases us in it pleased Whitman—pleased him, at least, in his old age. Perhaps the memory of his contributions to nursery morality still irked him. The sentence had his approval; he reflected with satisfaction that our squeamishness would be puzzled and offended by it, took it proudly to himself that he had been a sad dog in his day (there was always the gin punch after all), and probably hoped we should end by crediting him with sins of which he was innocent. The same miscalculated complacency appears in a letter which he sent to John Addington Symonds.

Referring, there, to experiences which left him the father of six children, he writes: "My life, young manhood, times South, etc., have been jolly bodily and doubtless open to criticism." Was any action of his life more open to criticism than the perpetration of this sentence? Our natural deduction from it would be that he was not only a sensationalist, but devoid of even the sensationalist's instinctive delicacy. Such an interpretation would allow nothing for the pride of the theorist or for the garrulity and forgetfulness of old age. The whole course of Whitman's life, the evidence of his relations and intimate friends, his freedom from any breath of slander (beyond what attached to him as the author of an "immoral book") show that he was at the furthest remove possible from the crude animal man whose conduct he sometimes seems to glorify. He is, on the contrary, of the shy, brooding, impassioned, devotional type, for whom sex, with all its ideals and reticences, lies at the core of being, so that impulsive trifling with its instincts would have affected him as a kind of moral suicide. We have to imagine a man—a man of a kind commoner, perhaps, in America than in England—who retains through life a girlish purity of mind and conduct, and though he ignores nothing, becomes at last more communicative in language and less consistent and discreet in action than the majority, because he has never made a certain kind of surrender and has preserved the fortress of his soul.

Whitman left New York in his twenty-ninth year, and taking with him his young brother Jeff, of whom he had constituted himself a kind of guardian, made a tour through the States on his way to New Orleans, where he was again to edit a paper. Throughout his life in New York, work at the desk, though always conscientious, had been no more than an exercise which his necessities imposed. He has been described as the idlest editor ever seen; and what really engaged his activities was the human spectacle, the majestic pageant, offered by the great city with its harbours and bridges and ships and thronging pavements. Time that was spent lolling among the wharfmen or hobnobbing with 'bus drivers was not lost time; for Whitman had those rare faculties which idleness instead of rusting ripens. There can be no doubt that his trip South was taken with conscious intention, that his new job attracted him because of the new contexts it would afford to his daily dreams and meditations.

This visit to the South, always associated

in his mind with the ecstatic and desolating history of his loves, became typical to him of the fusion of the Northern and Southern States into a nation, and seemed to give him the right to speak as representative of the whole. With him as with his country the fusion was achieved through agony and loss. Horace Traubel, the young friend of his last years, pointing one day to a photograph in the old man's room, was told it was that of " a sweetheart many, many years ago," but no further information was forthcoming. Talk ceased, Whitman looked out of the window, a new topic was started, and the silence in which he wrapped this phase of his career remains virtually unbroken. What facts are covered by it ?

Some of Whitman's admirers think of him as a man whose life was centred about one woman, a woman whom, through the prejudices of her family, he was prevented from marrying. Others suppose that his standard of morality was loose, and that free talk about sex went hand in hand in him with free action. Neither of these points of view seems likely to be the true one. No reader of *Children of Adam* or of any other of Whitman's deliverances on the subject of sex can fail to recognise that far from being free, they are dictated, in every line and word of them, by a scrupulous, a sometimes too scrupulous, conscientiousness. His point of view is that passion belongs and must be seen to belong to the life of the soul. It is because the paraphernalia and even the disturbances of sex have a spiritual bearing that he announces and recounts them. He was not of the type to sow wild oats; and in his maturity he certainly entered into no relations which did not seem to him as he entered into them to be in all their bearings spiritual.

But the problem so regarded becomes acuter; for faults of no principle are more easily explained or overlooked than faults of principle. What did his ideas of spiritual relationship include? Clearly they did not include irresponsible attachments. Throughout his writing upon sex, the procreative function is insisted upon; his lovers—'lovers' is not quite the right word for them!—are parents; and we can see that no life finally commends itself to him or comes really within his purview except that of the family. Yet, reading Whitman's poems and the various accounts that have been written of his life, I find it impossible to avoid concluding that, while he may only once have been deeply enamoured of a woman, his six children were not all the offspring of one mother, their father convincing himself, under the influence partly of his feelings, partly of confused theory, that, as an exceptional man, loved now by this woman and now by that, he could find and give an adequate conjugal love in more than one relationship. It seems to be generally admitted that the woman who touched him most nearly was of gentle birth, and rumour has it that silence as to his connection with her was exacted from him by her relations as a point of honour. Are we to suppose then that these strange relatives tolerated a recurring irregular connection while refusing a regular one? Whitman, we know, entertained at one time the bitterest feelings about the haughty and exclusive treatment to which he had been subjected. But is it certain that even when he became a lover he really contemplated marriage? "I once thought wedlock not needful to my development," he long afterwards confided to a friend, "but now I think that it would have been better for me." It is possible at least that love found him a dedicated Bohemian, and that what was exacted of him was that his unconventionality should remain anonymous. There is a certain kind of idealism to which the unreserving pledges of marriage appear as an affront; and Whitman, pledged already to transcendental union with his country, may have felt that the serene confiding joys of domesticity and its complete personal surrender must not be his. Whatever he felt, the woman who loved him would have felt also or striven to feel, and it may well be, therefore, that it was a certain pride of idealism that sundered them. All we know is that *Out of the Cradle Endlessly Rocking*, the world's supreme song of separation, is one of the all but earliest *Leaves*, and thus came from Whitman's heart immediately in the wake of the great wave of emancipated passion that launched his life-work.

But what, after all, must be the biographical interpretation of that incomparable poem? It was printed in the third edition of *Leaves of Grass*, the edition of 1860–61; Whitman first visited New Orleans in '49–'50. Now the intervening years, years in which all or almost all his most powerful songs were written, though they found him nominally at home in Brooklyn, are years of some mystery for his biographer. In a skeleton outline of his life, jotted down in old age, he lets fall two significant observations: "Have lived quite a good deal in the Southern States"; "Have visited, and partly lived in, most of the Western and Eastern cities." What is curious is that no record of any of these visits has come down to us. Mr. Bliss Perry, the poet's most recent and most authoritative biographer, has not a word upon them. And there seems no period of his life into which we can fit them, if we do not fit them into these years. Placing them then here, we bring one mystery into association with another and so, I think, in a certain degree illuminate both.

These unrecorded visits were, may we not suppose it? Whitman's enforced or chosen substitute for married life. How preserve the complete anonymity which we know to have been preserved, if not by passing freely from one town to another? Why leave no record of any of these visits and travels unless concealment were a part of their purpose? From the outbreak of war to the time of his death, it is quite clear that there is no woman in Whitman's life; and just before the war, he publishes that song which I have called a song of separation, but which is surely a song, not of separation only, but of bereavement. The gentleness, the desolation, the note of irretrievable blind searching for an object once so close and so dear, these and other touches in *Out of the Cradle Endlessly Rocking* point to a core of personal experience in it, for which a biographer must find some explanation. And the simplest, perhaps the only adequate, explanation is that it is the song virtually of a husband mourning for the death of one who was in all but name his wife. How else shall we account for its tender familiarities and our own irrepressible tears ?

There still remains the problem of his relation to his children. Mr. Bliss Perry, in the course of a long and never quite convincing list of analogies between Whitman and Rousseau, remarks that "each man wrote superbly about paternity and each deserted his own children." A charge so damning should not have been made, unless evidence could be produced to prove it. Mr. Perry does not seem to know more on this point than is known commonly. "Though unmarried," Whitman wrote to Symonds in the letter already quoted, "I have had six children—two are dead—one living Southern grandchild, fine boy, writes to me occasionally—circumstances (connected with their fortune and benefit) have separated us from intimate relations." The words suggest an understanding that money held in trust for certain children would be forfeit if their relation to Whitman became known; his action in holding aloof could not in that case be called desertion; indeed it is likely he would be himself the chief sufferer. Were these, however, the only children? The expression 'one Southern grandchild' suggests Northern grandchildren—

children, in other words, of Northern children. "Once," Whitman writes in a beautiful and yet a strangely disturbing poem :—

Once I pass'd through a populous city imprinting my brain for future use with its shows, architecture, customs, traditions,
Yet now of all that city I remember only a woman I casually met there who detain'd me for love of me,
Day by day and night by night we were together—all else has long been forgotten by me,
I remember I say only that woman who passionately clung to me,
Again we wander, we love, we separate again,
Again she holds me by the hand, I must not go,
I see her close beside me with silent lips sad and tremulous.

Must we then suppose that this faithfully loving son, comrade and brother could draw momentary sweetness from a relationship and lull himself with a memory, while the vital responsibilities it entailed fell upon the weaker partner ? There is nothing in Whitman's character to justify such a belief. If—as to me seems possible, probable even—some humble woman bore him a child or children (and whatever her station she would be his "ideal comrade," his "perfect equal") it would be consonant with what we otherwise know of him that she should seldom see him and know no more of him than that he was "Walt," but that he would leave her to struggle with the problems of maintenance unaided is a suggestion which, till it is substantiated, we may disregard.

It is important, in touching this side of Whitman, to leave no stone unturned. For to many readers nothing that we have said or could say would carry weight, if they suspected the existence of shady margins to which we preferred to make no allusion. If, it might be argued, *Once I pass'd through a populous city* is taken as autobiographical, ought not other poems, such a poem for example as *Native Moments*, to be taken in the same way ?

Native moments—when you come upon me—ah you are here now,
Give me now libidinous joys only,
Give me the drench of my passions, give me life coarse and rank,
To-day I go consort with Nature's darlings, to-night too,
I am for those who believe in loose delights, I share the midnight orgies of young men,
I dance with the dancers and drink with the drinkers,
The echoes ring with our indecent calls, I pick out some low person for my dearest friend . . .

Does not Whitman here, readers may ask, confess himself the most reckless libertine ? It will be the thoughtless reader who will ask the question. There are obvious distinctions between these two poems as biographical documents. The one recounts an experience, the other professes an aspiration ; the one has particularity, the other none. A man has only to become familiar with any sensation and its general aspects elude him ; the first impression becomes dulled and he revives it by fastening on points of more or less incidental detail. The implications of libertinage are pruriency, dullness, fatigue. *Native Moments* is full of freshness, zest and purity. It is ideal, rhapsodical. Some persons, happier or unhappier than their fellows, are perhaps constitutionally unaware what Whitman means by *Native Moments.* The poem is not for them. To those for whom it is intended, its aim and effect are somewhat of the kind that Aristotle claimed for Tragedy. It is a purge of passion. Certain elements of our nature become through the mere acknowledgment of them liberated ; they undergo a metamorphosis and lose their power and sting. There are things which if they can be said cannot be done, things done by those only who would be ashamed to speak of them. And so this poem. It is Whitman's substitute for, his vicarious enactment of, the deeds it celebrates. Instead of identifying him with those who through weakness degrade themselves, it removes him from them, while yet it is a link of sympathy deliberately forged and held, to bind them to him. The same purpose shows itself in such pieces as *To a Common Prostitute,* perhaps also in *Earth, my Likeness.* The last three lines of *Native Moments* are its best summing up :—

O you shunn'd persons, I at least do not shun you,
I come forthwith in your midst, I will be your poet,
I will be more to you than to any of the rest.

But let us return to the main outline of Whitman's career. He soon threw up his job in New Orleans, and, making on his way North a pilgrimage through what was at that time the West, penetrated to Chicago and the great lakes. His return home, after an absence of a year, found him still undecided as to the form which the great venture of his life was to take. He edited yet another paper, had thoughts of expressing himself by means of oratory and wrote, his mother said, " barrels of lectures." The instinct for personal expression was what ruled him, and a poet might have been lost to the world but for the fact that Walt had no gift of delivery. For some years he joined his father as a working carpenter, and built wooden houses, reading Emerson the while and thinking transcendentally. It was now at last that the conception of a new poetry began to define itself to him. He was already much more than a mere journalist, having contributed prose, and verse of the usual pattern, to the best periodicals of the day. When at last he set hand to the work with which the world identifies him, he went about his task characteristically, forming and maturing his style by dint of close, ruminative deliberation. The substance of his barrels of lectures was distilled into a dozen poems, and after four years a slender volume, *Leaves of Grass*, made its appearance.

Leaves of Grass was Whitman's presentation of himself to the world, and part of the impulse that produced it was a determination that, having been produced, it should go home. Expecting indifference or antagonism, he had in readiness three lengthy, explanatory, and laudatory notices of his work, which reputable journals published for him as anonymous reviews. Long afterwards reprinted in the volume of collected Personalia which was prepared under his direction and published by his literary executors after his death, they serve to give us a picture both of what he was in these days and of what he wished to appear to be.

> Self-reliant, with haughty eyes, assuming to himself all the attributes of his country, steps Walt Whitman into literature, talking like a man unaware that there was ever hitherto such a production as a book or such a being as a writer. . . . Of pure American breed, large and lusty, age thirty-six

years,—never once using medicine—never dressed in black, always dressed freely and clean in strong clothes—neck open, shirt collar flat and broad, countenance tawny transparent red, beard well-mottled with white, hair like hay after it has been mowed in the field and lies tossed and streaked. . . . No discontented—a careless slouch, enjoying to-day; no dilettante democrat—a man who is art-and-part with the commonalty and with immediate life . . . loves the free rasping talk of men—likes to be called by his given name and nobody at all need Mr. him—eats cheap fare, likes the strong-flavoured coffee of the coffee-stands in the market, at sunrise—would leave a select soirée of elegant people any time to go with tumultuous men, roughs, receive their caresses and welcome, listen to their noise, oaths, smut, fluency, laughter, repartee—and can preserve his presence perfectly among these, and the like of these.

It is all well enough. "First be yourself what you would show in your poem" is its motto, innocent of Milton, and neither to the self-consciousness of it nor to the complacency nor even to the self-advertisement need we demur. Yet a lack of fundamental coherency or squareness seems traceable. Self-consciousness, if pressed so far, should be pressed further; it should not refuse the last turn. Let Whitman if he will take leave of the select soirée and immerse himself in natural delights and the society of the tumultuous. To whom does he imagine his announcement of leave-taking to be made? The roughs would not be roughs if they took note of it; his remarks are really for the soirée, and postulate the audience they affect to despise. Literature is inevitably a divider of men, and from whatever source its roots draw sustenance, its fruit is for the few who have achieved some culture and enlightenment. Whitman persistently confused culture with the weaknesses to which it gives rise; and in the uncultured saw only the benefits accruing to them from their condition of latency. It devolved upon him to see and to declare more. We touch here upon a point of real insecurity in his character. He was without the discipline of education and under-rated or ignored its value. And so, in spite of his intellectual power, he misses the complete composure of the intellect. He wished to be, he wished also to present the appearance of being, a simple, natural man. And the incompatibility of these desires gave an assumed air to his indifference, touched his nonchalance with aggressiveness and plunged him into some egregious faults of taste. It is the climax when literature, the armoury of the mind, serves him with weapons for an assault upon itself.

The main fact about his first edition, printed and published by himself in 1855, was that it was read and understood by Emerson. But neither Emerson's appreciation, nor the author's puffing, nor even the modicum of really discriminating praise which it received from several American and English papers, sufficed to win a public for the book. Whitman, undaunted, sacrificed facts to appearances and brought out a second and enlarged edition in the following year. What more handy as a ram to breach the wall of public indifference than Emerson's generous words? "I greet you at the beginning of a great career. R. W. Emerson." stood in bold letters on the cover of the new volume; while, in an appendix, Whitman printed in full the now familiar letter from which these words had been extracted. The same appendix contained his astonishing reply:

> Here are thirty-two poems which I send you, dear friend and master, not having found how I could satisfy myself with sending any usual acknowledgment of your letter. The first edition, on which you mailed me that till now unanswered letter, was twelve poems—I printed a thousand copies and they readily sold; these thirty-two Poems I stereotype, to print several thousand copies of. I much enjoy making poems. . . .

and so on, a really nauseous mixture of perverted feeling and fact. Emerson passed the offence over, and we must do the like; but who can wonder that it became, in Whitman's circle, a point of bitter and futile questioning whether the sage of Concord had remained faithful to his first spontaneous verdict on *Leaves of Grass?* Whitman himself, who acknowledged the obvious debt and derivation of the book in printed homage to his Master,[1] went so far late in life as to contend that his knowledge of Emerson's *Essays* post-dated its appearance. Things personal and impersonal were indeed so subtly interwoven in his poetry that his conscience became confused on the subject. On the one hand, he could show greatness in his identification of himself with his book, as when he would attend some lecture of which it was to be the theme and bask visibly before a delighted audience in the praise the enthusiastic orator would lavish upon him. On the other, he could descend to trivial misrepresentations unworthy of a tradesman for the sake of producing impressions which, his work being what he believed it to be and what it was, might have been trusted to look after themselves. All

[1] Whitman's obligations to Emerson are indeed so obvious and so inclusive, that it has seemed unnecessary to enter into any discussion of 'sources' in this volume.

through life he continued to advertise himself through the press whenever opportunity occurred, debating anonymously the question whether or no the great American poet had arrived, and so forth; and in anticipation of death he spent several thousand dollars on the preparation of what he considered an appropriate mausoleum. Appropriate enough it is, except in the one particular of its origin, and perhaps he would not have had it otherwise. But I suppose there is no avowal on the monument that he erected it himself, and so, except to the few who know all, it either appears or is an imposture.

But to revert to his relation with Emerson. Anxiety for the reputation of *Leaves of Grass* never prejudiced Whitman's consistent love and reverence for him. Personal intercourse between the two was occasional but warm. Whitman was never quite at home in Emerson's company. We hear of him, when on one occasion he was Emerson's guest, calling out for beer to be brought in a tin mug, a tiresome piece of democrat's self-consciousness. But the celebrated talk on Boston Common ideally summarises their intercourse. There experience, sagacity and compromise encountering obstinacy and intuition found more than their match. "'What have you to say then to such things ? ' said Emerson, pausing in conclusion (Whitman's poems of sex had been the theme). ' Only that while I can't answer them at all, I feel more settled than ever to adhere to my own theory and exemplify it,' was my candid response. And thenceforward I never wavered or was touched with qualms (as I confess I had been two or three times before)."

This talk took place in 1860, Whitman having gone to Boston to see his third edition through the press. Its nominal publishers were Thayer and Eldridge, but the book retained, as Whitman's books always continued to do, as much of his personal shaping as was compatible with printed pages. *Children of Adam* and *Calamus* now first took their definite place in his scheme ; and with one or two notable exceptions the great songs which together give *Leaves of Grass* its impact and momentum had all been composed. This Walt, whose lazy ways and neglect of the main chance his family with tolerant affection deplored—for he missed a boom in the building trade in Brooklyn in the early fifties—has in these ten years heard and justified the final call, has claimed and secured a place among the masters of the world's literature. But the period in which he is to live primarily the poet's life, short as it has been, is almost over. In April, 1861, came the outbreak of the Civil War.

The war was the test of Whitman's character, and the heroism it evoked in him throws a compelling splendour of light backwards and forwards over the whole course of his days. Some have professed surprise that he did not volunteer for service in the ranks, or have thought it necessary to allege the streak of Quakerism in his blood. But a poet, like a general, has conflicting duties in war-time; indeed it is a point of military virtue that he should not needlessly expose his person. Whitman felt it his duty to determine not merely what he could do but what he could do best for his country. And it fell to his lot in the end not so much to risk death once as to die daily. He surrendered his life drop by drop, and the survivor of the war, though he survived it by nearly thirty years, was a mutilated veteran.

Instinct, which time has proved to have been inspiration, told him that he, of all men, could provide for the great struggle its imaginative theatre. So late as November, 1863, when he had been already over a twelvemonth in the wards, he wrote to his friend Charles Eldridge, "I feel to devote myself more and more to the work of my life, which is making poems. I must bring out *Drum Taps.* I *must* be continually bringing out poems." His brother George had volunteered for service with the Union troops; down South, linked, we may suppose, if not identified with the Secessional cause, were other hearts with which his own could not but beat. He remained at home during the first eighteen months of the struggle, and it was there that a large part of *Drum Taps* was composed. At last, hearing that George had been wounded, he set out for the front, and, once among the scenes of the war, found his high and rarefied poet's consciousness engulfed and obliterated before daily and hourly calls upon his common human sympathies. "During my two years in the hospitals and upon the field," he wrote from Washington to *The New York Times* in December, 1864, "I have made over six hundred visits and have been, as I estimate, among from eighteen thousand to twenty thousand of the wounded and sick, as sustainer of spirit and body in some slight degree, in their hour of need." Supporting himself by ill-paid secretarial work in a Government office, he devoted all his energies to nursing (of which he had already had some experience among his friends the 'bus drivers in New York), spending as much as seven hours a day in the wards, and not giving up, though his health was repeatedly threatened, so long as a single wounded man was left in Washington. Any cash he could put by (his own wants were confined now and always to the bare necessities of life), and any he could collect from friends or acquaintances, went to provide for the soldiers those small luxuries and comforts which he knew did more than anything to suggest the atmosphere of recovery. Sometimes, after consultation with the doctor, there would be an "ice-cream treat" for a whole ward; but as a rule he would bring a variety of small trifles, chosen to meet the whims of various patients and make them feel that they were remembered—for this man an apple, for that a stick of candy, and so on; and never, while funds lasted, were his capacious pockets without their supplies of stamps, writing paper, and above all, though he was not himself a smoker, of tobacco. This was action on an heroic scale; but perhaps no one but Whitman could have supplemented it with the last and most endearing touch. It is beautiful that the poet should become a nurse; it is still more beautiful that the nurse should not forget he is a son. All through the strain and preoccupation of his work, Whitman never failed to find time for a weekly letter to his mother.

These letters, long afterwards published under the title of *The Wound-Dresser*, should be read by any who doubt Whitman's claim to a place in the communion of saints. Tenderness and devotion are of course predominant features in them :—" I believe no men ever loved each other as I and some of these poor wounded sick and dying men love each other"—but perhaps their most noteworthy quality is the complete self-possession they display. Fully aware of the momentous nature of the events which are passing on every side of him, Whitman is never betrayed into a touch of false fervour; never exaggerates any of his feelings by a hair. He turns quite naturally from tragic narrative to take his part in the small cares of the daily life of the family :—

> Well, Mother, I should like to know all the domestic affairs at home; don't you have the usual things eating, etc? Why, Mother, I should think you would eat nearly all your meals with Mat. I know you must when they have anything good (and I know Mat will have good things if she has a cent left). Mother, don't you miss *Walt* loafing around, and carting himself off to New York toward the latter part of every afternoon?

Or again, on a more serious topic :—

> What to do about Andrew I hardly know—as it is I feel about as much pity for you as I do for my

poor brother Andrew, for I know you will worry yourself about him all the time. I was in hopes it was only the trouble about the voice, etc., but I see I was mistaken, and it is probably worse. I know you and Jeff and Mat will do all you can—and will have patience with all (it is not only the sick who are poorly off, but their friends; but it is best to have the greatest forbearance, and do and give, etc., whatever one can—but you know that and practice it too, dear Mother).

Then, from the same letter as the last :—

As there is a limit to one's sinews and endurance and sympathies, etc., I have got in the way, after going lightly, as it were, all through the wards of a hospital, and trying to give a word of cheer, if nothing else, to every one, then confining my special attentions to the few where the investment seems to tell best, and who want it most. Mother, I have real pride in telling you that I have the consciousness of saving quite a number of lives by saving them from giving up—and being a good deal with them; the men say it is so and the doctors say it is so—and I will candidly confess I can see it is true, though I say it of myself. I know you will like to hear it, Mother, so I tell you.

After so much assumed arrogance, how beautiful, how completely reassuring is this unassumed humility!

We expect a poet to be vague and emotional in his benevolences, and could forgive him if he were so. Whitman is not. A remarkable symptom of his power is the range of attention he had for minute detail in the wants and feelings of his innumerable patients.

"I find more and more," he wrote to a friend who was helping him, "how a little money rightly directed, the exact thing at the exact moment, goes a great ways. To make gifts comfort and truly nourish these American soldiers, so full of manly independence, is required the spirit of love and boundless, brotherly tenderness, hand in hand with greatest tact."

Among his thoughtfully chosen offices was that of writing letters for the soldiers to friends and sweethearts; and in the case of death, he would often write, on his own account, to the parents in the unknown home:—

MR. AND MRS. HASKELL,[1]—Dear Friends, I thought it would be soothing to you to have a few lines about the last days of your son Erastus Haskell, of Company K 141st NY Vol. . . . I think he was broken down before he came to hospital here—I believe he came here about July 11th—I took to him. . . . I used to sit by the side of his bed generally silent, he was opprest for breath and with the heat, and I would fan him . . . Sometimes when I would come in he woke up, and I would lean down and kiss him, he would reach out his hand and pat my hair and

[1] The quotations are from a long and detailed letter about the case; see "Traubel," *With Walt Whitman in Camden*, p. 115.

beard. . . . I shall never forget those nights, in the dark hospital, it was a curious and solemn scene, the sick and wounded lying all around, and this dear young man close to me, lying on what proved to be his death-bed. I do not know his past life, but what I saw and know of he behaved like a noble boy. . . . Poor dear son, though you were not my son, I felt to love you as a son, what short time I saw you, sick and dying there.—But it is well as it is,—perhaps better. Who knows whether he is not better off, that patient and sweet young soul, to go, than we are to stay? Farewell, dear boy,—it was my opportunity to be with you in your last days,—I had no chance to do much for you, nothing could be done—only you did not lay there among strangers without having one near who loved you dearly, and to whom you gave your dying kiss.

Looking back on it, Whitman gave the war a significance for his literary development which it had not really possessed. In a farewell essay he writes that "without those three or four years and the experiences they gave, *Leaves of Grass* would not now be existing," and by an arrangement which violates chronology he has made *Drum Taps*, which contains indeed some of his most moving and memorable passages, the pivot of his book. He regarded himself and we regard him as peculiarly the poet of the war; yet, as we have seen, the bulk of his most characteristic expression preceded it. He was, indeed, always more sensitive to truth of principle than to accidents of fact; and the truth here was that the national feeling which found its expression in the war had in him been strong enough to anticipate such an expression, so that, when the war came, the poems which it might have evoked were written already, leaving their writer at liberty to enact them, and to exhibit in his own person a supreme poem of comradeship and love. Nothing that left Whitman's hand after the war has quite the old unquenchable and intoxicating bravura of independence, and we often feel him striving for the effects he does not reach. But the power on which those old frenzies were stayed has been revealed to us; we recognise in his message a greatness which only devoted action could fitly crown.

Whitman lingered on in Washington some years after the war was over, having obtained permanent employment under Government as a clerk with a salary which by '66 had risen to 1600 dollars (£325). It was in this year that his superior, a Mr. Harlan, finding, it is supposed, a copy of *Leaves of Grass* in the poet's desk, was shocked by it and dismissed him. Matthew Arnold, writing to W. D. O'Connor in acknowledgment of his torrential manifesto, *The Good Gray Poet*, "doubted whether here too, or in France, or in Germany, a public functionary would not have had to pay for the pleasure of being so outspoken the same penalty which your friend has paid in America." But nothing cooled the ardour of a panegyrist, who—it is well to remember—had, in earlier days, opened his home to Whitman and could yet regard him as a simultaneous reincarnation of Homer and the Christ. Whitman was soon reinstated in another branch of the service and his dismissal became an advertisement of his work. The tide was in any case beginning to turn. Even Arnold, who deplored his eccentricities, acknowledged his abilities, and so did every other English critic of consequence. His name was also beginning to be widely known in Europe. Mr. W. M. Rossetti's selection from *Leaves of Grass*, published over here in '68, was received so warmly that Whitman's serene Americanism wavered. Feudalism had accepted him, freedom had not; and there was a tinge of reproach as well as of perplexity in his triumph. Perhaps he forgot that his countrymen had not enjoyed those reconciling discretions which Emerson recommended but Rossetti enforced.

Whitman's Washington period (he did not

vacate his post till '73) is one in which, mainly through his letters to his mother and to the young tram-conductor Doyle whom he treated as his adopted son, he becomes for the first time a perfectly familiar figure. From this time forward we can follow him in all his daily doings, and it is curious to observe that the effect of this familiarity is to make us more deeply aware of his personal aloofness. We recognise that his daily life, whether in work or idleness, is the deliberate expression of some motive power which lies concealed. The reason for this is perhaps twofold. On the one hand, we are for the first time observing his actual personality by the side of the assumed personality of the hero of *Leaves of Grass*, and find to our astonishment that the man is greater than the book, and different from it; in fact, that he is its complement. And then, his natural aloofness as a man is emphasised by the fact that he is conscious of having emptied his great reservoirs and is endeavouring to refill them. His personality does not overflow with the abundant expressiveness characteristic of previous years; he is content to pass his "heyday," to "range the high plateau" of his life, at the desk in a Government office.

The strain of the war had culminated for

him in the assassination of Lincoln, for whom, through occasional glimpses of his " careworn face " from Washington pavements, he had come to feel deeply. When the news reached him he was at home recruiting his strength, and his great lament was wrung from a heart already strained almost to the breaking point. That noble tribute would, otherwise, have been still nobler. Years passed, but the strain never lifted. He produced notable work, among other things the splendid prose prophecy *Democratic Vistas*, and poems, like *Passage to India*, which, if less convincing in *élan* than their predecessors, show a continually deepening spiritual consciousness. But the achievement of his middle age was to be that of patience under suffering, the acceptance of premature diminishment.

In January, '73, trouble culminated in a slight paralytic stroke. In May of the same year his mother died, and, the grief and shock overwhelming him, he found himself physically prostrated. " Pete, my darling son, I still think I shall weather it, but time only can show," he writes in July, " Mother's death is on my mind yet, time does not lift the cloud from me at all " ; and, a month later, " I have the feeling of getting more strength, and easier in the head—something like what

I was before Mother's death—I cannot be reconciled to that at all yet—it is the great cloud of my life—nothing that ever happened before has had such an effect upon me." So he passes into the slow and difficult years of an eclipse from which he is never fully to emerge. But he writes as faithfully to his "darling Pete" as he had written earlier to his mother, and makes out of this very ebb of his power material for one or two of the sublimest of his poems. Have any doubted his fundamental integrity of soul? They see him now subjected to the last tests, and proving himself against them victoriously. "A batter'd wreck'd old man," he identifies himself as he loved to do with another discoverer of a New World, and in *Prayer of Columbus* thus communes with and reports himself to his Maker:—

Thou knowest my years entire, my life,
My long and crowded life of active work, not adoration merely;
Thou knowest the prayers and vigils of my youth,
Thou knowest my manhood's solemn and visionary meditations,
Thou knowest how before I commenced I devoted all to come to Thee,
Thou knowest I have in age ratified all those vows and strictly kept them,
Thou knowest I have not once lost nor faith nor ecstasy in Thee.

The spirit of the words, no more the aggressive "Here I am" of his first confessions, lifts into higher contexts the unassuming candour of his letters home.

Have any questioned, again, the solidity of that *rapport* with Nature of which, in his early poems, he made so much? He tells us that in early life all his reading—spasmodic, but wide, and calculated to acquaint him with most of the masterpieces of the world's poetry and philosophy—had been conducted in the open air and within sound of the sea, and attributes to this the fact that he remained self-poised through those great doses of vicarious experience. The experience of Nature had been, we are to understand, his touchstone of reality. He had tested his own work by confronting it with the sea, the hills and the grass of the prairie. But was there, after all, a touch of affectation in that worship of the wild, so loudly heralded? The hushed voice of the paralytic in *Specimen Days* silences every doubt. "Timber Creek," the retreat to which for two summers Whitman daily tottered and where, from sun and stream, sitting in the shade of the old oak or wrestling with the hickory saplings, he bit by bit drew strength and movement to his crippled limbs, deserves, more than his self-erected monument, to become a place of pilgrimage, perennially associated with his name :—

> In this dull scene, (as most folks would call it,) why am I so (almost) happy here and alone ? Why would any intrusion, even from people I like, spoil the charm ? But am I alone ? Doubtless there comes a time—perhaps it has come to me—when one feels through his whole being, and pronouncedly the emotional part, that identity between himself subjectively and Nature objectively which Schelling and Fichte are so fond of pressing. How it is I know not, but I often realise a presence here—in clear moods I am certain of it, and neither chemistry nor reasoning nor esthetics will give the least explanation. All the past two summers it has been strengthening and nourishing my sick body and soul, as never before. Thanks, invisible physician, for thy silent, delicious medicine.

The great English poet who wrote that "Nature never did betray the heart that loved her" leaves us, through a certain desiccation that visited his old age, wondering whether the love of nature he advocates had in fact the persisting value he claimed for it. For Whitman the society of hills or of trees contained nothing which was not contained in ampler measure in the society of human beings; and its virtue was that it revealed, with slow cumulative emphasis, truths which the hum of affairs often obscures from us. He felt no contrast between nature and humanity; he felt merely that certain emotions which give life its unity of tone and are implied in all experience, may come home to the soul more simply and therefore more convincingly under the stars or within sound of the " mystic surf-beat of the sea." He loves nature not because it is more, but because it is less, than man and, being less, displays with greater clearness the enduring and yet elusive outlines of the truths of the spirit. So, when he is too infirm to find nourishment in the strong meat of human intercourse, he turns to Earth, to Earth in her homeliest aspects, and drinks in a forsaken marl-pit the milk of his convalescence.

From the point of view of our present study, Whitman's last years may be dismissed as uneventful. They were full of such incident as belongs to circumstances at once public and retired. They show him beautifully making the best of a life in ruins and at the end dying heroically. Their story is too simple and too familiar to need more than the briefest recapitulation. He passed them partly in his brother George's home at Camden, Philadelphia, partly in a small house of his own in the same small town, chosen not for its amenities—it seems to have possessed none—but because trains and trams were within hearing and there was a lilac bush in the yard. While with his brother, Whitman had a room on the top floor from which he hobbled down to meals. George was not a kindred spirit, "preferring pipes to poems," but the lonely old man liked the atmosphere of a family, and when Walt, his little namesake, died, felt it more than the child's parents. As his health improved he made various excursions—to Canada with his disciple Dr. Bucke, to St. Louis to see his brother Jeff, and out West as far as Denver and the Rockies. He still felt himself to be America in epitome. The great plains of Missouri exhibited anew to him the measureless "eligibilities" of which he had been a prophet, the tumult and splendour of the mountains gave him the law his poems had obeyed. More soberly, he assumes the rôle of national spokesman, "wafting in America's name" messages to our shores on Tennyson's birthday or at Carlyle's death, celebrating the murder of Lincoln annually with a public lecture, and giving, as occasion arose, sympathetic and discerning estimates of the scope and quality of his fellow-craftsmen.

Gradually he became in Camden the centre of a small coterie of enthusiasts. A man cannot be a mark for pilgrimage and attract no attention locally. Whitman attracted even his Boswell, and entered with zest into quite a variety of schemes which aimed at laying the principles of *Leaves of Grass* and its author's personality before the world. All this is tedious, and it led to the formation of a spurious atmosphere about the man. He tells his young biographer Traubel on no account to " prettify " him and to put all the " hells and damns " into his conversation ; he puts some in himself perhaps, so that Traubel may have them to put in afterwards ; in brief he sees that he is getting a halo and is not quite so irreconcilable as he would appear. But if there is an element of lingering self-absorption and amiable weakness in his decline, these traits, once fairly acknowledged, do nothing to affect the noble continuity of the outline of his life ; and we should be poorer but for the last apostolic babblings. Even the trivial indulgences, the garrulity, of the old boy are acceptable parts of our picture of him. For sustaining and enclosing all, his courage, his spiritual rectitude, the spontaneous pleasure with which, as his field of consciousness narrows, he welcomes all that it still discloses to him, are as it were his signature and ratification of the legacy with which he has enriched the world.

BIOGRAPHICAL

Whitman's life illustrates, perhaps in a unique degree, that fusion of the physical and the spiritual which is the prevailing theme of his poetry :—

> Mélange mine own, the unseen and the seen—

he writes in his strange jargon ; and how can we but find in his fate a type and symbol of the ideas he stood for ? From the beginning a trace of esoteric mysticism is discernible in his work ; he has in him that strain which, if he choose to develop it, will lift him above and away from his fellow-men, to pursue and perceive arcana. Is it that the material ties prove too strong, or is it through the promptings of some still deeper sanity ?—whatever the cause, he bends his visionary power upon the common things of life, its routine, its machinery, its universal pleasures, and through them reaches out to that spiritual world of which he is intuitively assured. Possessing perfect health as a young man, he proclaims health to be the chiming of the soul with the universe through the bodily instrument ; but from the first he is conscious that the meaning of life, thus viewed, appears only when its richness and variety are related to the enclosing fact of death. He intends *Leaves of Grass* to present the poetry of life and death in equipoise. The equipoise is given otherwise than he intended and more intimately than he knew. The book exhibits his crippled faculties in their slow decay, while yet to the last word the unconquerable spirit keeps its integrity and purpose. Then, finally, he writes the poetry of death, like that of love, in the convincing characters of his example.

II

THE PROBLEM OF THE FORM

"*His rhythm and uniformity he will conceal in the roots of his verses, not to be seen of themselves, but to break forth loosely as lilacs on a bush, and take shapes compact as the shapes of melons or chestnuts or pears.*"

SALIENT among the problems with which Whitman and his work confront us is that of the form in which his poetic impulse clothed itself. To what extent are his Leaves a natural and coherent growth? To what extent are their shapes vital shapes? And how are we to discern what is vital in them from what is trivial or redundant? To answer these questions involves analysing, however cursorily, the relation of the form to the matter in poetry as a whole. It is arguable that the highest kind of poetry rejects a rhythmical plan or predetermined scheme of any kind: that its form can be determined by nothing else than the creative impulse which takes as it arises the form proper to it. The attainment of poetry will in this view be the attainment of complete freedom. Can any one believe that the true poem is dependent for its unity upon preserving an equal number of stresses in a line or lines in a stanza? Its unity lies surely in the fact that it proceeds from a continuously developing emotion; and this, as it grows to the light, will open here a leaf and there a tendril and here again a bud or a flower, all unpredictably and each in shape and size responsive to the various degrees of light that fall upon it, adaptable to no pattern. So Walt Whitman must have argued; and some of the greatest monuments of emotional literature exist to assure us that he was not wrong in believing that the essence of poetry overflows all its moulds. His *Leaves of Grass* was a deliberate challenge to the conventional ideas of what is beautiful and appropriate in verse.

What to such as you anyhow such a poet as I? therefore leave my works,
And go lull yourself with what you can understand, and with piano-tunes,
For I lull nobody, and you will never understand me!

It is a bracing if not a reassuring note. Whitman in fact challenged so much that we shall do well to search for the residue left unchallenged by him. What is the ground common to him and other poets?

THE PROBLEM OF THE FORM

The poet uses language and summons before our minds, as language must do, an array of thoughts and images, his object being to communicate the feeling which these thoughts and images arouse in him. The feeling sometimes includes and transcends the thought and imagery, sometimes merely insinuates itself among the thoughts, touching their surfaces; however that may be, it is more for the sake of the feeling than for their own sake that the thoughts and images are presented; the feeling is the determining principle, the creative centre of the work. Shelley's

> Hail to thee, blithe spirit,
> Bird thou never wert—

is not a piece of perverse ornithology. It denies a fact in order to establish an emotion. And to guard it against a literal interpretation, the denial is couched in a peculiar form; it is made rhythmically.

If a friend is with me and I use the expression "How delightful!" he can gauge at once from his knowledge of my character and from the tone of my voice what kind of delight I am experiencing and how much of it; but the words, printed upon the page of a book, suggest no more than that some unknown person has experienced an unknown quantity of a feeling of which we know no more than that he thought or professed to think it pleasant. Now the problem in poetry is to find some substitute for the tone of the voice. The printed symbols are to be redeemed from dumbness and so ordered that we shall recover in them the quality of the poet's mood, the breath and emphasis of his expression. They are to be the embodiment, not the mere record, of his experience. We are to find in them the unique spiritual impulse out of which they came.

To convey this organic effect poetry falls back upon something more primitive than words. Birds and animals communicate their feelings to one another by variations of tone which the whole fraternity recognises and which we ourselves can recognise to have a direct significance. Besides varying the tone they express themselves also by varying the rhythm of their cries. That highly-strung creature, the blackbird, conveys excitement in screams which are not only shrill but also punctuated and distributed in an expressive pattern. The coo of the turtle-dove in its unflagging persistency and that of the wood-pigeon in its soft retarded pressures would express, even without help from the quality of the notes, that brooding domesticity which is characteristic of both these birds. Not only the tone of the voice, then, but, as we see by these primitive examples, its rhythm also, assumes a natural impress from the feeling of the utterer. It follows that in so far as words can be made rhythmical, their rhythm, as dictated by the poet's feeling, will convey to us immediately as we hear it, the feeling which it is his purpose to convey.

So far we have Whitman with us whole-heartedly. His native instinct for rhythmical expression is indeed abnormally powerful.

> I behold from the beach your crooked inviting fingers,

he writes of the sea in his first great poem, and the rhythm of the line beckons of itself unmistakably. A little later we have

> Cushion me soft, rock me in billowy drowse,

and the rhythm lulls now and assuages. Effects like these are common in *Leaves of Grass*, and a great part of the pleasure it gives us depends upon them. Differences arise when we go further and consider the conditions under which language and rhythm are best associated. In poetry we have as a rule not only rhythm but metre—a measurable something which is common to one line after another, one stanza after another, a uniform pattern which underlies their subtly varying forms. Why is this ? If rhythm is an immediate expression of feeling, we might have expected rhythm and feeling to change obviously together, as, in *Leaves of Grass*, they actually do. Putting aside our experience of poetry and habit of mind in regard to it, we see that its regularity is a curiously artificial product and calls for explanation.

The explanation is to be looked for in the nature of the rhythm in words and the limitations and difficulties imposed by it upon the poet's art. One of the commonest fallacies of the prosodist is that of supposing that our normal pronunciations are susceptible of precise metrical analysis ; that certain syllables are long, definitively, and certain other syllables definitively short. On the contrary, the problem of prosody is to strike averages ; not to discover the length of syllables, but why and how it is convenient for certain purposes to regulate or conventionalise their length. When we speak with feeling, we here dwell on a syllable or on a word, there run rapidly forward, crowding a number of unimportant words or syllables together. We do this easily and naturally ; and we can do it because words have no strongly inherent rhythm of their own. Their meaning as words does not depend upon the length of time it takes us to pronounce them. And so far as their relation to feeling goes, they are indeterminate matter. They do not dictate a rhythm to us; the more intense our feeling, the more natural we find it to dictate to them, and to no matter what combination of them, any rhythm we will. Feelings, in live speech, are in fact irrepressible, and can safely be left to declare themselves after their own fashion.

This being so, the tendency of language has been to consider clearness and practical convenience in the formation and articulation of words, so that we may be provided with a medium for the accurate exchange of information and ideas. Here then is the poet's difficulty. The purposes of language are opposed to his purposes. For the expression of his feeling he must find in words and make to appear from within through his use of them the rhythms which feeling ordinarily forces upon them from without. Like the pigeon or the blackbird, he feels a certain measure or pulsation appropriate to the emotion he has to convey; but in order to convey it he must find words to suggest it, and how is this to be done? The emotion which we convey in speech takes its own rhythm and pulls the words this way and that to make them fit it. In poetry the rhythm of the emotion must somehow find its embodiment in the words so that as we read the words we recognise the rhythm and feel the emotion. And since the same words are susceptible of different rhythms according to the emotion we put into them, how is it possible for us to arrive at the poet's rhythm and emotion through his words ?

In brief, when we see a line of poetry before us, to what is due our confidence that we feel its rhythm as the poet intended it to be felt ?

> A child said *What is the grass?* fetching it to me with full hands ;
> How could I answer the child ? I do not know what it is any more than he.

If we ask half a dozen of our friends to read this aloud to us, we shall probably find that to each of them the four clauses have a slightly different shape and cadence. In particular the value of the words *said, is, to, me,* in the first line will be variously interpreted, while, in the second, rhythmical ambiguity will extend to as many perhaps as eleven syllables. For example, we may read :—

> Hów could I ánswer the chíld ?

or :—

> How could Í ánswer the chíld ?

or :—

> Hów cóuld I ánswer the child ?

and again :—

> Í do not know what it ís any more than hé

or :—

> I do not knów whát it is ány móre than hé

or :—

> Í do not knów what it ís any móre than hé.

and so on almost indefinitely. Our disposition at first will be to assure ourselves that this perplexity is fictitious ; that to discuss the rhythm of the lines is academical ; that the version which seems most natural to ourselves is the correct one. Let me place my own version before the reader as a test :—

> A chíld sáid *Whát is the gráss?* fétching it to me with
> fúll hands ;
> Hów could I ánswer the child ? Í do not know what it is
> any more than hé.

I must not flatter myself he will accept it. And though I have marked where, to my ear, the stresses fall, I may still have failed to convey to him what seems to me to be the cadence of the lines. Now uncertainty of this kind is, in varying degrees, unavoidable where the rhythm is free ; that is, where each line is its own law and pattern. And yet, unless the rhythm is communicated with exactitude,—wherever, that is, the poet fails to make clear to his reader what cadence he intends,—the words are liable to lose their poetic quality and to become lifeless. It is here that metre can assist us; as a rhythmical scheme separable from the words and exemplified in them it provides a basis for mutual understanding.

Now the more mutual understanding is set up between the poet and his reader, the wider, the more resourceful becomes, clearly, the poet's vehicle of expression. Reflecting again upon the lines of Whitman just quoted, we observe that our uncertainty as to their exact rhythmical intention is hardly distinguishable from our uncertainty as to the exact shade of meaning he intends them to convey. What does this imply? It implies surely a great sacrifice of expressive power. For if the subtleties of a poet's rhythm are only appreciable as the result of an appreciation of the subtleties of his meaning, it is clear that they cannot contribute anything to that meaning on their own account. But when the rhythm follows a plan, we take its broad outlines for granted; it is something known; and this means that we have attention to spare for the turns, the syncopations, the irregularities, which contribute so much to its expressiveness.

Again, the effect of a regular rhythm, perhaps as a result of its directness and immediacy, is very soon played out; and to sustain it, to keep the attention, variations must be introduced. The language of rhythm, in its more developed phases, involves (as every musician knows) a constant play of anticipation and surprise. Effects are produced, meanings are conveyed, by preparing the mind to expect one thing and giving it another. Hardly is a rule laid down before, now in one, now in another direction, it is disregarded. And it is in these variations, this embroidery, that the value of rhythm as a medium of progressive communication really consists. But, obviously, if you are to depart from a rule, you must have a rule to depart from. Variations imply a theme. The significance of the irregularities is their deliberate and measurable deviation from a recognised basis of regularity. It is to metre, then, that the poet turns for a basis of regularity against which his irregularities may play. Without it, he is limited to the broadest outlines for his rhythmical expression, to shapes that will impose themselves on the unguided attention; and even these broad outlines will often be ambiguous. For subtler play of rhythm he will be obliged to fall back upon the relation of sound to sense, and, instead of adding rhythmical to linguistic effects, derive the one from the other.

Thus the first question which criticism has to answer in regard to the form of Whitman's poems is this : how far in discarding metre did he reckon with the value of what he discarded ? how much intelligence and craftsmanship, how much technical experience lay behind his choice of spontaneous methods ? This decided, we shall be able to ask to what extent his apparent irregularities conceal an order equivalent to that attained in the conventional regularities of other poets.

A curious feature of *Leaves of Grass* is the frequency with which lines of a conventional pattern are introduced in stanzas which, as stanzas, are completely free. The hexameter is quite a favourite ; elegiac couplets several times occur ; the ordinary blank verse line is, of course, the commonest of all. More than this, even rhymes are resorted to occasionally. The natural tendency of criticism is to take these manifestations as a tacit admission by the poet, only the more significant if it was unconscious, of the virtue of the forms against which he was in rebellion. Mr. Paul Elmer

More even goes so far as to say that the " prevalent effect " of *Leaves of Grass* is " that of a hexametric cadence such as probably preceded the schematisation of the Homeric poems," and his opinion clearly is that the perception and acknowledgment of this by Whitman himself would logically have involved him in a similar schematisation of his own work. But Mr. More exaggerates the relative frequency of hexameters, even if we include under that heading a generous measure of hexametristic lines. And his view of Whitman generally is hardly sympathetic enough to reveal to him the positive grounds on which Whitman's rejection of common forms was based. Sometimes, no doubt, a sort of instinct for formal composition takes Whitman, as it might seem, at unawares ; he has written one or two splendid poems in which the quality of his inspiration appears to demand from him a consistent flow of rhythm, and only habit, it might be argued, leads him to refuse this. Some of the most majestic lines in *Prayer of Columbus* and *Song of the Universal* take a familiar pattern :—

Shadowy vast shapes smile through the air and sky.

or :—

Love like the light silently wrapping all,

and these poems, with a few others, might, perhaps, be called metrical in their entirety, examples of a frustrated and magnified blank verse. But I know of no poem which can fairly be said to imply the hexameter as a base. And, in the compositions just alluded to, it must be noted that the magnificence of the verse is bound up with its frustration. If the *Song of the Universal* is great, its theme makes it so; the versification is fumbling, and descends more than once into a merely metristic prettiness. Indeed the poem, in spite of its beauty and triumph at the close, is a laboured piece of work. The opening paragraphs, in particular, betray a weak search for adventitious decoration, a feature which is of all others the most uncharacteristic of *Leaves of Grass* as a whole. Lines like

> As from tall peaks the modern overlooking,
> Successive fiats absolute issuing,

would have been enough to destroy a lesser poem, and their weakness lies precisely in their relation to a norm; they have so far demeaned themselves as to become Iambics! Thus even those poems which come nearest to metre owe their strength to their disdain of it.

As a general rule the appearance in his work of the waifs and strays of rhyme and rhythm has a disquieting effect. They are momentary, miscalculated ebullitions. Children of fashion that have lost their way they are jostled by the Bohemian crowd, which bestows upon them and receives from them unkindly glances.

Thou Mother with thy equal brood,
Thou varied chain of different States, yet one identity only,
A special song before I go I'd sing o'er all the rest,
For thee, the future.

Could any passage be more accurately calculated than this to give displeasure? The trivial skipping motion on a hackneyed idea in the second line, the meandering complacency of the third line,—first wilful violation of a rhythm we have been led to expect, then foolish insistence on a rhythm which is not worth having when we have got it,—all these things are bad enough to prepare us for the worse that follows. The pity of it too is that the disorder, the clash of poetry, pedantry, and piano-tunes, is enjoyed, deliberately aimed at. The opening lines of the *Song of the Broad Axe* are another flagrant example :—

Weapon shapely, naked, wan,
Head from the mother's bowels drawn,
Wooded flesh and metal bone, limb only one and lip only one,
Gray-blue leaf by red-heat grown, helve produced from a little seed sown,
Resting the grass amid and upon,
To be lean'd and to lean on.

Half concealed by wayward printing, we have here in effect an eight-line stanza, in which the lines are all equivalent and all rhyme together. The one or two touches in it of descriptive genius, the beautiful use of the word 'wan', are not enough to redeem the whole from absurdity; and again we must note that the absurdity has been sought out, enjoyed. Another poem, which begins in high declamatory style :—

And now gentlemen,

lets us down after a little into the lamest jog trot :—

Having studied the new and antique, the Greek and Germanic systems,
Kant having studied and stated, Fichte and Schelling and Hegel,

hexameters as worthless, as meaningless as, once more, they are intentional. Turn even to that noble threnody, *When Lilacs Last in the*

Dooryard Bloom'd, and on the very threshold a sheer barbarism confronts you :—

> Ever-returning spring, trinity sure to me you bring.

What does this betray if not a childish, under the circumstances a fatuous and even wanton, pleasure in a silly jingle of words ?[1] There is no

---

[1] After long turning over in my mind, tasting and re-tasting, the tercet of which this is the first line, I have come to suspect in it a concealed rhythmical intention which would make such harsh terms unjustifiable. The line at first sight scans :—

> Éver-retúrning spríng, trínity súre to mé you bríng,

and in this form is, to me, anathema. Yet Whitman, who could write a line like :—

> Will you not little shells to the tympans of temples held . . .

cannot complain if readers attribute to him other barbarisms. The true scansion of the tercet seems, however, to be this :—

> Éver-retúrning spríng, | trínity súre to me yóu bríng, |
> Lílac blóoming perénnial | and dróoping stár in the wést, |
> And thóught of hím I lóve. |

There is, that is to say, a sequence of five members, each of them bearing three accents ; and these trinities of accents are, I suppose, a conscious symbolic reinforcement of the idea of the trinity of recollections. The whole conformation of the stanza would, according to this reading, be the result of scrupulous and delicate adjustments ; and the purpose of the opening rhyme might be to prepare the reader's attention for an unusual effect. As a further instance of what looks like conscious moulding to a norm, it may be observed need to multiply examples. Clearly Whitman's refusal of metre was the refusal of innocence, not of experience. One must doubt whether his ear was capable of receiving the disciplined music of such verse as Milton's, whether, in fact, the verse of all the greatest poets did not seem sing-song to him. Certainly, whatever determined his choice of irregularity, his perception of the meaning of conventional forms, his instinct and practice in the use of them, were at a primitive level. He is far from being unsusceptible to the charms of metre. But they are Circe charms to him. Crying out for an ideal of nonchalance and ease he escapes a temptress.

It is true of all commanding poetry that its form is only perfect when it is secondary, when it is an instrument, a vessel :—

> The words of the true poems give you more than poems . . .
> They do not seek beauty, they are sought,
> Forever touching them or close upon them follows beauty,
> longing, fain, love-sick.

---

that the rather curious accentuation "su′re to me you bri′ng" is echoed at the transition between the next two members very beautifully ("-e nnial and dro op-"). But the uncertainty attaching to all this is instructive. Whitman seems to be trying here to obtain effects to which a scheme is indispensable. And it is a good instance of the risks of metrical antinomianism that it should permit so much care to be directed to communicating what after all remains obscure.

To none does the truth apply more accurately than to Walt Whitman's. The echoes of cultivated verse exercised a considerable influence upon him, and this influence, as far as it went, was damaging. His own wild music, ravishing, unseizable, like the song of a bird, came to him, as by his own principles it should have come, when he was not searching for it. And his greatness as a poet, when we regard his poetry on its formal side, is that conventional echoes damaged him so little, that in spite of unavoidable elements of wilfulness and reaction in his poetry, he was able to achieve so real an independence.

Independence, it is necessary to remember, was in his case essential to artistic success. For he had to find the forms which would be appropriate to a specific purpose. He set out to discover a means of direct personal appeal, capable of ranging from the levels of a merely conversational tone, familiar but always ardent, along the broad and copious lower slopes of vivid description and specification, and up by the steps and steeps of impassioned argument and persuasion to those heights of prophetic ecstasy and assurance where speech itself is a song. And this he actually achieves. He gives us poems which represent severally all the different stages of the ascent; he gives us other poems—and these perhaps are the most characteristic of him—in the course of which we pass imperceptibly from one stage to another, now rising, now falling as the development of the theme requires.

In all, the determining condition of the form is this direct personal impulse. The poem, as Whitman conceives it, is to remain fundamentally a conversation. It is to be the expression by me to you of the feelings which are as much yours as mine, and would undoubtedly have been expressed by you to me but for the accident of my being the more garrulous fellow of the two. It is to act in the field of spiritual needs much as the more modern kind of advertisement does in the field of material needs, button-holing its client, assuring him that he is a brother, and confiding to him its knowledge of the common perplexities of the life of man. How easily this atmosphere of confidence and familiarity raises a smile! It subsists largely upon illusions; but the illusions are harmless, for they deceive nobody; and they are really worth entertaining, even if they are a little wearisome and over-persistent at times; for with them come large reinforcements of that genuine raciness and diffused good feeling which are part of America's contribution to the civilisation of the world. There was more of strength and perception and courage than there was of weakness in Whitman's determination to turn this unpromising stuff to poetic uses. The impromptu confab, in which equal takes equal aside for a few words (or not so few!), this he felt to be typical not only of his country but also of his country's ideals. And it is in poems where a conversational tone is the most apparent that he is most completely himself.

As I lay with my head in your lap camerado,
The confession I made I resume, what I said to you and the
    open air I resume,
I know I am restless and make others so,
I know my words are weapons full of danger, full of death,
For I confront peace, security, and all the settled laws,
    to unsettle them,
I am more resolute because all have denied me than I
    could ever have been had all accepted me,
I heed not and have never heeded either experience,
    cautions, majorities, nor ridicule,
And the threat of what is call'd hell is little or nothing
    to me,
And the lure of what is call'd heaven is little or nothing
    to me,

Dear camerado! I confess I have urged you onward with
me, and still urge you, without the least idea what is
our destination,
Or whether we shall be victorious, or utterly quell'd and
defeated.

It is tempting at first sight to argue that this, being mere prose, would be more sensible and straightforward as a continuous paragraph. Little, indeed, seems to be added to the composition by the scanty formalities in virtue of which it claims the name of a poem. But the question is not whether there is much or little, but whether there is enough. For what, after all, is the artist's essential quality, if not to know how much exactly is enough and to give no more? "O," sings the forsaken mocking-bird, with whom Whitman identifies himself in perhaps the loveliest of his poems :—

. . . O I think you could give me my mate back again if
you only would,
For I am almost sure I see her dimly whichever way I
look.

"I am *almost* sure I see her *dimly*"; that quaver of uncertainty in the words is the source of their power. The sentimentalist would have been quite sure he saw her clearly, and would have demanded instant restitution! Only passion can afford to take gradations, to admit its doubts. The poem *As I Lay* exemplifies power of a similar kind. The theme resolves itself into a series of autobiographical reflections; yet, in their total effect, these reflections touch us intimately; and the effect, so far as form contributes to it, results from the fact that we have been asked to stray upon the borderland of prose and poetry by a guide confident of his power to keep us on the right side of the border.

The beauty of the poem, formally, is that it is content to hang its existence upon a thread. Each line is a single contributory thought floated to us on a contributory breath. The single impulse which produced the whole has divided itself into a succession of waves of impulse, which vary in height and volume, each, whether by sympathy or by contrast, affecting the height and volume of the rest. Take one instance only of the workings of these subtle compensations: who can read the words "Dear camerado" at the beginning of the last line but one, without an instinctive recovery of the cadence of the first line of the piece, with the blending emotions of intimate affection, calm concession, confiding resignation, which were expressed in that and the line following? The intervening lines, it is equally obvious, have been, as waves, a kind of complementary reaction. The tide has been stationary; there has been a retirement, a back-wash. But the water as it continues to move continues to prepare us for a new pressure of advance; and in the last two lines this new pressure has arrived. Swiftly and smoothly it spreads over a fresh stretch of sand and leaves us at the end with an exquisite sob or falter as, in its completion, it disappears.

Dear camerado! I confess I have urged you onward with me, and still urge you, without the least idea what is our destination,
Or whether we shall be victorious, or utterly quell'd and defeated.

We must note further as an essential feature of the form at which Whitman is aiming that each poem he writes has to be judged by an intrinsic standard. Most of the conventional forms with which we are familiar have their fixed possibilities and limitations; to adopt the sonnet form, the *In Memoriam* quatrain or that of Omar Khayyám, is to entitle the reader to more or less specific expectations, and he will judge a poem written in these metres according to the degree in which it fulfils what he expects of them or replaces his expectation by something better. The form of Whitman's conversational poem depends on the course the conversation takes and the temper which has initiated it; and whether the form is perfect or not in a particular case we can decide only by familiarising ourselves with the unique requirements of the case in point. Thus, in the example that follows, the tone of conversation has passed into that of soliloquy; the mood is too intimate, too remote, to admit of the idea of any but an impersonal utterance; we picture the soul of the poet addressing as it were some shadow of itself:—

Tears! tears! tears!
In the night, in solitude, tears,
On the white shore dripping, dripping, suck'd in by the sand,
Tears, not a star shining, all dark and desolate,
Moist tears from the eyes of a muffled head;
O who is that ghost? that form in the dark, with tears?
What shapeless lump is that, bent, crouch'd there on the sand?
Streaming tears, sobbing tears, throes, choked with wild cries;
O storm, embodied, rising, careering with swift steps along the beach!
O wild and dismal night storm, with wind—O belching and desperate!
O shade so sedate and decorous by day, with calm countenance and regulated pace,
But away at night as you fly, none looking—O then the unloosen'd ocean,
Of tears! tears! tears!

The form here is of such exquisite sensitiveness that it is with an effort we remember the offences its author could commit. The lines "O who is that ghost" and "What shapeless lump is that" serve just to maintain the air of realistic familiarity that Whitman loves. He takes advantage of the ballast they provide to soar up into heights of suggestion and impressionism where he is equally at home. The storm, the human creature out in it, exchange forces, appearance, personality almost, from line to line. The tears are the rain, but who is it that is weeping? The night, the tempest, the seashore are part of the solitude and the despair they cover, part of the outpouring of passion and sorrow which they liberate, echo and absorb. And how does language take the impress of hints so vague and so conflicting and of an integration so profound? All through the piece alliteration, though never obtruding itself, and indeed never appearing till it is sought out, adds significance to the choice of the words by coaxing the reader to dwell upon them and so helping him to pass naturally over gaps whether of grammar or idea which might otherwise check him; he may observe next how every line, sensitive to the cadence of the first, divides itself sympathetically into a succession of lesser impulses, of which there are usually, but not always, three; and finally, as the sign of a still more vital sensitiveness, he will note the repetition of the keynote of the piece, the word "tears." The word is not only repeated, but variously placed in successive lines, so that by maintenance of the emphasis upon it its structural significance may be fully brought out. Then, at what is structurally the centre of the piece, there is a cessation; four lines of release and tumult follow which are silent of it; and so we are prepared for the beauty and inevitability of the final cadence in which it returns.

In *Tears! Tears! Tears!* we have a piece of poetic architecture which is at once completely original and completely satisfying. To measure the achievement it represents, let us oppose to it an example of merely conventional melodiousness. Here, from Spenser's *Teares of the Muses* (a poem which extends to 600 lines), is the first verse of the mourning of Melpomene:—

> O who shall powre into my swollen eyes
> A sea of teares that neuer may be dryde,
> A brasen voice that may with shrilling cryes
> Pierce the dull heauens and fill the ayer wide,
> And yron sides that sighing may endure,
> To waile the wretchednes of world impure?

A passage like this brings vividly before us a vicious tendency to which verse-writing is subject even in the hands of true poets—when the form evokes rather than expresses the feelings of which it is the mould. To call the tendency vicious is not to deny that it sometimes produces exquisite poetry, if never poetry of a kind which Whitman would have recognised. And though he would have been wrong to see nothing but artifice and insincerity in it, these are, nevertheless, besetting dangers. Let any reader, who will deal strictly with himself, turn the pages of his most cherished master ;—how many works will he find of which he can say that their form, however appropriate to the feeling, completely fills it, that nowhere a line, a phrase, a word has been inserted for form's sake ? The sincerer our devotion to poetry, the more readily we recognise that even in works called great, the form is apt to be a convenient mantle which, though it serves indeed to reveal the living gestures of the poet, serves also to give an average effect of dignity to transitional moments, when he is recovering from one gesture and preparing for the next. Form, as Whitman made use of it, avoids this pitfall. Not pre-existing as a mould to be filled, it cannot attract the feeling that is to fill it. It waits upon the feeling, and the feeling when it comes is the more likely to be genuine and sincere.

Hardly, however, are we free of one snare before another has us. Does it follow because a feeling is sincere that its expression is of value or importance ? Obviously not. A poet may be mistaken in his estimate of the interest and vitality of some moment of seeming inspiration ; and the artifices of form which were but lately his temptation become now his test and his guide. For the structural conformities to which he pledges himself impose upon him, as it were, a minimum standard of intensity, a qualitative pattern, to which his feeling, if it is to unify and justify itself, must rise ; and thus they give both to himself and his readers a rough standard by which to judge externally of the strength and value of the poetic impulse. At times, then, metre may tempt the poet to produce mere formalities or to mistake formalities for forms, but at other times (and these the more frequent) he will be protected by it against the dangers of a formless emotionalism.

Here precisely is Whitman's point of weakness. Unconfined, he is also unsustained. Accepting no conventional necessities, he can surrender to aimlessness what he has vowed to freedom. Poet of the inexpressible, he can forget that though expression fails when thought has been transcended, it also and more usually fails because thought has been neglected or faultily applied. The 'leaf' following is typical of but too many even among those that belong to the period of his maturity :—

A leaf for hand in hand ;
You natural persons old and young !
You on the Mississippi and on all the branches and
bayous of the Mississippi !
You friendly boatmen and mechanics ! you roughs !
You twain ! and all processions moving along the streets !
I wish to infuse myself among you till I see it common for
you to walk hand in hand.

The intrusion here of the Mississippi, with its branches and bayous, is something quite inexplicable ; and the flowing rhythm of the line, its conscious alliterations and repetitions, emphasise the intrusion and make it ludicrous. From the line "You twain ! and all processions moving along the streets" one might fairly infer that there is a kind of procession in America that is called a "twain" ; possibly that is the case. The whole piece is neither individualised nor universalised, neither seen nor thought ; and it is the informality of the writing that makes its incoherence possible.

The same sort of incoherence involves some of the longer poems in disaster. Perhaps the most desperate case is that of the *Song of the Exposition.* Man's conquest of the material world in his arts, crafts, sciences, manufactures is endowed in this laboured recitative with all the lustre of a spiritual attainment of which the most to be said is that material conquest makes it possible. The show takes place in a glorified Crystal Palace,

High rising tier on tier with glass and iron facades . . .
Bronze, lilac, robin's-egg, marine and crimson,

and this palace is to add an eighth to the seven wonders of the world ; while the Muse herself,

Bluff'd not a bit by drain-pipe, gasometers, artificial fertilizers,

settles herself down in the midst of the monstrous brood and promises to be at home. The poem is indeed a series of crying discrepancies between thought and form. A rudimentary sense of humour, courageously called in to fill the breach, merely reveals its gaping amplitude. " One stately house," the assurance is gravely accorded to us :—

One stately house shall be the music house,
Others for other arts—learning, the sciences, shall all be here,
None shall be slighted, none but shall here be honor'd, help'd, exampled.

Throughout the piece a noble idea writhes and torments itself in the effort to dignify an inappropriate occasion. In vain Whitman acknowledges and even vaunts the more uninspiring details associated with his theme. His ecstasy does not interpenetrate with them ; his manifest labour is so great that it is no surprise to find him in one passage completely losing touch with his own thought :—

To you ye reverent sane sisters,
I raise a voice for far superber themes for poets and for art,
To exalt the present and the real,
To teach the average man the glory of his daily walk and trade,
To sing in songs how exercise and chemical life are never to be baffled,
To manual work for each and all, to plough, hoe, dig . . .
For every man to see to it that he really do something, for every woman too ;
To use the hammer and the saw, (rip, or cross-cut,) . . .
To work as tailor, tailoress, nurse, hostler, porter,
To invent a little, something ingenious, to aid the washing, cooking, cleaning,
And hold it no disgrace to take a hand at them themselves.

How beautiful, what a reflection upon the rest, is the first line of this pathetic descent into imbecility ! The mental shuffle which occurs at the words " To manual work "— where the word " to " is taken up imitatively in a sense which the grammar and the thought equally refuse—gives the signal for a general stampede of the faculties. Why specify of the saw that it must be rip or cross-cut? How invent without ingenuity or aid the washing without taking a hand? And then, alas! what an air of self-congratulation in the rhythm of the last line! At the climax of the poem sense and grammar are again sacrificed for the sake of a rapture which even so is not attained:—

> Now here and these and hence in peace, all thine O Flag!
> And here and hence for thee, O Universal Muse! and thou
> for them!

What form except Whitman's would have enabled an artist to flounder so hopelessly among the shallows, now plying fins, now wings, and ignorant all the time whether he is on land or in the water or the air? [1]

Whitman's failures, numerous as they are, do not affect his stature as a poet. His successes, and the fact that his successes include some of the longest and most audacious of his works, suffice to establish his power in conception and creation and the quality of his touch as an executant. Among his greatest gifts is his command of the music of words,

[1] It is only fair to remind readers that the *Song of the Exposition* was composed by request for use at a public ceremony at a time when the condition of Whitman's health made sustained effort impossible to him.

the freedom with which he can throw off phrases equally remarkable for their significance and for their beauty. And it is worth noting here that the free structure of his work enabled it in a peculiar degree to accommodate the concentrations of poetic motive to which this gift gave rise. We know how the vague films of the oyster shell are knitted into a pearl under the influence of a creature vaguer, filmier than themselves. Similarly in Whitman, poetry is, on the one hand, diffused, a nourishing, penetrating fluid, a living milk; on the other hand, it is always ready to crystallise itself at need; and the two conditions, instead of destroying, seem naturally to explain and support one another. His form, not demanding a poetical manner from him, is not cast down by the appearance of the jewel of poetry when occasion brings it forth, but is ready, exists in fact, to provide a natural setting for it.

> O baffled, balk'd, bent to the very earth,

he cries out, in one of his most solemn moments, using accents and entering with them into an atmosphere that recalls the religious illumination and self-effacement of an Ezekiel or an Isaiah. In all but the next line he is

> Aware now that amid all that blab whose echoes recoil upon me I have not once had the least idea who or what I am.

And how can we but wonder that in these two utterances, apparently so different in tone, a community of substance and feeling should announce itself! The fact is indubitable. Both take their place in a paragraph permeated, irradiated, by the splendour of its opening line.

The intrusion of what is ordinarily called form would make transitions of this kind, with the action and reaction, the underlying principle of compensation they involve, impossible. Nor need we go outside Whitman's own work for proof of this. In *Pioneers*, *Dirge for Two Veterans* and elsewhere, he has endeavoured to combine his familiar thought and method with a concession to formal regularity. The result is always the same. The thought loses its distinctive flavour. Something has clouded and adulterated the flow of a stream which was only delicious to us when its waters were absolutely pure.

> The moon gives you light,
> And the bugles and the drums give you music,
> And my heart, O my soldiers, my veterans,
> My heart gives you love.

There is little enough form, one might suppose, in such a stanza; and yet there is enough to raise a doubt about the aptitude, the connection, the value even, of the sentiments which are expressed in it ; there is enough to give the expression of love it contains an appearance of insincerity, to expose it as trivial in fact, while it affects to be solemn. The cause is simply clumsiness, inexperienced handling. And we must remark that *Dirge for Veterans* would be condemned to failure if only because of its resemblance to one of Whitman's ordinary ' leaves.' It has the same apparent carelessness of manner, the same apparent disconnectedness of the materials brought together to form the picture, the same iteration of each detail till its significance for the whole is grasped. It has in fact all the features so appropriate and so necessary in a leaf of grass so inappropriate and so superfluous in a wreath of flowers. The phrases in the poem which should have been pearls—for instance, that wonderful description of the full moon looking down upon a new-made grave—

> The sorrowful vast phantom moves illumin'd,—

these, instead of lending their poetry to their surroundings, are robbed by their surroundings of the poetry inherent in them, and must be torn from their setting if they are to be appreciated.

This is but another way of saying that Whitman in the bulk of his work had found by intuition the form which his genius required. His conception of poetry, his poetic habit, demanded, on the one side, spontaneity; they demanded, on the other, universal simplicity and receptiveness. The forms of poetry are artificial. Language submits to discipline in order to assume them, and disciplined language cannot express spontaneous feelings. The appearance of spontaneousness can only be obtained by an allowance for the requirements of the form, by an imaginative effort so perfect that we are unaware it has been made. This involves a certain conventionalisation of the feeling to be expressed. Most of the shades, the hesitations, the convergences, the conflicts of impulse have to be obliterated. The tentative processes of growth escape, as it were, through the meshes of the measured line and stanza; what these give to us is the clear movement and outline which, when the growth is achieved, represent and announce its characteristic features. There is a sense, obviously, in which such handling was beyond Whitman's scope; there is a sense also in which it was not good enough to attract him. His nature was too crude for poetry; but it was also too sensitive; poetry was, in a sense, too crude for him. One of the most perfect of his compositions takes for its theme a metaphysical, an elusive, yet for all that a very familiar emotion—*The Terrible Doubt of Appearances*—and the poet reaches his climax of perplexity in the amazing line :—

> Maybe seeming to me what they are (as doubtless they indeed but seem) as from my present point of view, and might prove (as of course they would) nought of what they appear, or nought anyhow, from entirely changed points of view ;

This heap of stumbling contraries, this litter of words, this rubble of ideas, is in its place pure poetry. Whitman's point is to express the disorder, the commotion of feeling which accompanies a certain confusion and distress of the mind, to express the state of reasonable, of seemingly final, uncertainty, before which philosophy itself becomes powerless, and to express this in such a way that having felt it we may also feel its resolution :—

> To me these and the like of these are curiously answer'd by my lovers, my dear friends,
> When he whom I love travels with me or sits a long while holding me by the hand,
> When the subtle air, the impalpable, the sense that words and reason hold not, surround us and pervade us,
> Then I am charged with untold and untellable wisdom, I am silent, I require nothing further . . .

Everything in the piece, every word and detail, every repetition and parenthesis, every concession and modification, is part of a single effect; and the effect, when we have it, is an effect of beauty, a revelation of life in its conditions and inner principle, a picture of spiritual growth and conquest. All depends upon Whitman's fearless use of a form which aimed primarily at the expression of gradations, and which rejected set patterns as too clumsy to admit of faithfulness to the imperceptible ebb and flow and interplay of vital emotion.

III

THE FORM (ii)
CONSTRUCTIVE PRINCIPLES

OUR understanding of Whitman's form is incomplete till we see what it excludes; for a thing has no positive if it has no negative qualities. Of course the idea of *Leaves of Grass* was to be all-inclusive; the poem was conceived in a spirit of universal hospitality, and such a spirit would be unfavourable to conscious method of any kind, would be likely to pride itself on having none. But this more or less inevitable pose must not bluff the critic. The form of a work which aims at impressing us with the spiritual coherence of all things may well share the elusiveness of its theme and be as inapprehensible as life itself. Yet unless some connecting thread, however fine, holds its divergences in a unity, the aim is unaccomplished.

Form in verse means, as a rule, metre. Whitman felt rightly that no metre or combination of metres could serve the peculiar purpose he had in view. At the same time he was not averse, as we have seen, to the introduction of metrical fragments here and there, and even shows a partiality for jingling effects. If we are right in thinking that he made a mistake in this, we have only to analyse the grounds on which our judgment rests, and we shall find the principle of exclusion which we are looking for.

But first let us note that the mistake itself was of secondary importance. The primary requisite for the form of *Leaves of Grass* was that its spaciousness should be recognised and that the composer should write to scale. No one afflicted with sensitiveness about the minor literary proprieties would have been likely to rise to the careless amplitude of manner necessary to the filling of so gigantic a mould. We recognise this easily enough if we compare the master with his followers, the originator with the mimics. The normal writer of Whitmanesque verse feels in every line the influence of the metre he has dispensed with and exhibits the affectations of a disdainful culture. But Whitman, like all who bring a revelation through art, is faithful to nature, and his method turns upon the discovery of nature in what had seemed unnatural. He aimed at being himself in his poetry, and this required him to stand out as poetry personified in solitary relief against the whole poetic achievement of the past. He seemed to ask less than others of the Muse. It devolved upon him to give more. Choosing informality, he chose in effect a form which permitted him no concealment, no breathing-space. We cannot wonder if he did not stay to consider what his ideals denied to him; his task was to be ready with what they exacted. Only the intrusion, the conspicuous and abiding presence of matter inconsistent with the common forms could justify his departure from them.

Yet if he rather transcends than refuses metre, it is not the less true that recognisably metrical lines are out of keeping with the spirit of his poetry. His lines are not metrical; what are they, then? We glanced earlier at an objection often taken to the form of *Leaves of Grass* to the effect that it has a spurious emotionality; that the line-system has the same relation to poetry as the habitual use of italics has to prose. The objection, we think, is inapplicable; but obviously the presentment of a composition in lines is meaningless and otiose, unless the lines have some common measure and are identities in nature as well as in name.

The identity of the lines in metrical poetry is an identity of pattern. The identity of the lines in *Leaves of Grass* is an identity of substance; and this is in effect by far the subtler and more exacting condition of the two. Tyrannous spontaneity allows the poet so little respite that every line must, as it were, contain his personality in the germ. Whitman himself never, I think, formulated this demand, and in the course of his work he frequently overrides it. But it is a natural deduction from his admitted principles. He looked upon each of his poems as the leaf or branch of a tree. The line is to the poem what the poem is to the work as a whole. To say this is to say that certain forms are excluded, that certain kinds of line will not do.

A quotation from early manuscript passages written before Whitman had quite found his bearings will show better than anything else what his form rejects and why. Among the variorum readings given in the third volume of the Camden Edition of the collected works (p. 128) we find the following:—

> There is no word in my tongue,
> No array, no form of symbol,
> To tell his infatuation
> Who would define the scope and purpose of God.

Readers familiar with *Leaves of Grass* will at once feel a want of equivalence in these four lines; and what does the sensation point to if not to the presence of equivalence in Whitman's lines generally? Each true line of Whitman's comes to us, as I have said, floated separately on an independent breath. Like the sea-waves to which he himself so often compared them, his lines are not less recognisably units because of their variable shapes and sizes. And in the third of those quoted above, some principle of equivalence is violated. It is violated, therefore it exists. The words "to tell his infatuation" are merely transitional; they explain what precedes, prepare for what follows, and offer the mind no substantial resting place. The passage as it continues becomes still more instructive:—

Mostly this we have of God: we have man.
Lo, the Sun:
Its glory floods the moon,
Which of a night shines in some turbid pool,
Shaken by soughing winds;
And there are sparkles mad and tossed and broken,
And their archetype is the sun.

Of God I know not;
But this I know;
I can comprehend no being more wonderful than man;
Man, before the rage of whose passions the storms of heaven are but a breath;
Before whose caprices the lightning is slow and less fatal;
Man, microcosm of all Creation's wildness, terror, beauty and power,
And whose folly and wickedness are in nothing else existent.

The weakness here is quite as obvious, if not quite so transparent. In the first passage one of the lines was like a plank bridging a chasm over which the reader walked insecurely, feeling as if there were nothing under him. Here the effect is of a succession of stepping-stones. The lines are independent, but they are discontinuous. And the reason soon appears. The observations of the first stanza are not really made for their own sake; they are made with a purpose: in fact, in order to prepare us for a simile. Even their independence, therefore, is apparent rather than real. It is not independence; it is insulation. The turbid pool, the soughing winds, do not appear before us substantively; they are counted out like symbols, and each has its stage in the process of ethical deduction in which the simile is applied. The lines that hold them are, in fact, dependencies; they are not full lines; they demand their unit of attention from us and do not satisfy it.

It is to the junction in them of these two seemingly incompatible qualities, continuity and independence, that Whitman's mature lines owe their integrity, and it is this that dictates their behaviour in company, so to speak, explaining the shape of the poems, their formal development, and the difficulties and resources of the craftsman. The line is a personality, the poem is a battalion, the book is an army. To illustrate the point, let us quote a paragraph in full :—

Here is the efflux of the soul,
The efflux of the soul comes from within through embower'd gates, ever provoking questions,
These yearnings why are they ? these thoughts in the darkness why are they ?
Why are there men and women that while they are nigh me the sunlight expands my blood ?
Why when they leave me do my pennants of joy sink flat and lank ?
Why are there trees I never walk under but large and melodious thoughts descend upon me ?
(I think they hang there winter and summer on those trees and always drop fruit as I pass ;)
What is it I interchange so suddenly with strangers ?
What with some driver as I ride on the seat by his side ?
What with some fisherman drawing his seine by the shore as I walk by and pause ?
What gives me to be free to a woman's and man's good-will ? what gives them to be free to mine ?

The importance of continuity to the form is displayed at once here in that *epanaphora*, that taking up of words or phrases, which is a pronounced characteristic of the style of *Leaves of Grass*. Each line hangs by a loop from the line before it. The motion is like the motion of walking; we continually catch up our foremost foot and take a half step beyond. It is of course the substantial self-sufficiency of the lines that necessitates this interlocking. And their equivalence turns upon their relation to a progressive, an accumulating idea. For example, the repetition of such a phrase as "the efflux of the soul," though it lengthens the line in which it occurs, does nothing to help that line to take us further; it has a different function; it joins the line more closely to its predecessor than the pronoun "it" would do and, by demanding less attention from the reader, decreases the weight of the line, thus actually preserving the equivalence it seems at first sight to impair.

In what sense, then, finally are the lines

> Here is the efflux of the soul

and

> The efflux of the soul comes from within through embower'd gates, ever provoking questions,

equivalent lines? We have seen that their equivalence is in their content; to say this is to say that it is in their context also—that it depends upon their association together. They have not the equivalence that two lines of blank verse have and which they have equally whether they stand next to one another or not. The second is equivalent to the first only as consequent upon it. In the first, an image is, as it were, posited: the conception of the soul as a radiating centre. In the second, the same image is elaborated. Suppose then that for the second line, stumbled at first sight by its length and complexity, we substitute

> The efflux of the soul comes from within through embower'd gates,

and stop there, we shall find, not only that the line has lost poetry, but that it has lost equilibrium also. Why is this ? Surely because, in the line as Whitman wrote it, we take the phrase

> comes from within through embower'd gates

transitionally, and because it is when so taken that its true value appears. If we emphasise it, as would be necessary were it to stand alone, we lose its suggestiveness and go searching for some precise significance which we do not find. But if we pass by way of it to the words

> ever provoking questions

and look to them for the first purpose of the line, the phrase falls into its relative place with beautiful accuracy. Is it because the gates are embowered that the questions are provoked ? This, or something like it, gives the line, no doubt, its coherence of idea. But the point is that a mystical and an everyday expression have been weighed together and that their effect is felt in their juxtaposition.

We weigh them in this way together because they are placed before us as constituents of a single line ; and, having so weighed them, we find that the momentum set up by

> Here is the efflux of the soul

is preserved and carried one stage further. The equivalence of the two lines is thus an equivalence of movement and of weight.

The problem of each succeeding line will be the same; to preserve the movement, to advance it by a stage and to maintain equilibrium in the advance. Reading to the end of the paragraph with this idea in view, we shall find that each line solves the problem in its own way. One has an element of surprise, another brings us into closer contact with the object, a third has its expanding generalisation, a fourth its illuminating detail ; and the line in parenthesis is especially noticeable, niched there like some light obstacle in flowing water and revealing the current which it checks. To put the matter in general terms : the constitution of a line in *Leaves of Grass* is such that, taken in its context, the poetic idea to be conveyed by the words is only perfectly derivable from them when they are related to the line as a unit ; and the equivalence of the lines is their equivalent appeal to our attention as contributors to the developing expression of the poetic idea of the whole.

Thus the progress of Whitman's verse has much in common with that of a musical composition. For we are carrying the sense of past effects along with us more closely and depending more intimately upon them than is possible in normal verse. What we can achieve at any point of our structure depends upon the trains of association we have set up, the number of balls we have kept spinning, the speed and quality of movement we have attacked or attained. And just as the context limits, so it also lays its claim upon us. For if no line can do more than maintain and add its unit to the general flow, none may do less. And just as in music, so here; it is impossible to lay down any rule for the maintenance of equivalence of effect, for the retaining of attention and accumulation of interest to the close. The condition of the effect that we are to produce now is the effect we have produced up to now; it lies with the modifications we have produced in our hearer's receptivity, the anticipations we have formed there. Here a *fortissimo* seems necessary; but its place is taken perhaps by a *pianissimo*, perhaps by a silence, and the effect is sustained. There we have a *diminuendo;* its point lies in the *crescendo* that preceded it; and behold! while the sound lessens, the meaning grows. Throughout, the test is whether the emotional pitch propounded is maintained, whether the piece continues to expand in significance as it expands in volume.

Perhaps it is because the significance of words accumulates faster than that of notes of music that frequent division into paragraphs becomes necessary, and also the frequent interpolation of parenthetical reflections. We go back and begin again where we began before in order, not that we may travel the same route a second time, but that we may travel to the same goal by a neighbouring route:—

Allons! whoever you are come travel with me!
Traveling with me you find what never tires.

The earth never tires,
The earth is rude, silent, incomprehensible at first,
Nature is rude and incomprehensible at first.
Be not discouraged, keep on, there are divine things well envelop'd,
I swear to you there are divine things more beautiful than words can tell.

Allons! we must not stop here,
However sweet these laid-up stores, however convenient this dwelling we cannot remain here,
However shelter'd this port and however calm these waters we must not anchor here,
However welcome the hospitality that surrounds us we are permitted to receive it but a little while.

These lines exhibit splendidly the alternating *crescendo* and *diminuendo* spoken of above. In " Traveling with me you find what never tires " we come immediately to a climax; there is no carrying the idea further; we must have a line of silence and start afresh. " The earth never tires " takes up the idea again, and in a sense is an addition to it; but it is a concessive, an explanatory addition; it is a concrete example and suggestion, and, as such, is taken as platform for a new " flight into the wordless." The poet soars, using a marked *crescendo*, which comes freely because the theme is simple. The line " I swear to you " is an easy and yet an enjoyable *fortissimo*. Again there is a pause; and then a new theme develops (the transitoriness of life on earth), needing tenderer handling; and so we have the deliberate and delicious *diminuendo* which brings the paragraph to a close.

The use of parenthesis is a recurring feature of Whitman's technique, and no explanation of his form can be adequate which does not relate this peculiarity to the constructive principles of the whole. He frequently begins a paragraph or ends one with a bracketed sentence, or begins or ends some section of a poem with a bracketed paragraph, sometimes even begins or ends a poem parenthetically. Thus the

Song of the Exposition opens with the beautiful aside :—

> (Ah little recks the laborer,
> How near his work is holding him to God.
> The loving Laborer through space and time.)

and the last piece in *Calamus* significantly closes :—

> Be it as if I were with you. (Be not so certain but I am now with you.)

This persistent bracketing falls well into the scheme we have laid down of independent units that serve an accumulating effect. The bracket, one need not remark, secures a peculiar detachment for its contents ; it also, by placing them outside the current and main flow of the sense, relates them to it in a peculiar way. And although for the time being the flow is broken, it by no means follows, as we saw, that our sense of the flow is broken ; on the contrary, it is probably enhanced. We look down upon the stream from a point of vantage and gauge its speed and direction. More precisely, the bracket opening a poem or paragraph gives us, of course, the idea which that whole poem or paragraph presupposes, while the closing bracket gives the idea by which what precedes is to be qualified and tempered. We have thus as it were a poem within a poem ; or sometimes, when a series of brackets is used, we have a double stream of poetry, as in *By Blue Ontario's Shore* where the waters blend and yet remain discriminate, a deeper and more personal current of feeling persisting under the strength and buoyant onrush of the surface. All this carries out and amplifies the peculiar formal significance of *Leaves of Grass*, with its strange submission of words to unfamiliar musical associations. Continuity and independence being Whitman's opposing principles of composition, independence emerges in the bracket into relative prominence. The disjunctive spirit of language asserts itself; literature contemplates music.

But the analogy with music is still unexhausted. Not only is the method of progression similar, the means of progression have also much in common. The chief difference between musical and verbal expression, as a rule, is that words, carrying each their modicum of meaning, have done their part when they have delivered it, while notes, being meaningless except in combination, develop new meanings by presenting a single combination in varying contexts or with varying accompaniment. In fact, repetition, which the artist in language scrupulously avoids, is the foundation and substance of musical expression. Now Whitman, for reasons we have touched on, uses words and phrases more as if they were notes of music than any other writer. As we shall see elsewhere, it was to him part of the virtue and essence of life that its forms and processes were endlessly reduplicated; and poetry, which was delight in life, must somehow, he thought, mirror this elemental abundance. Language generally expects us, when an object has been mentioned, to hold that object in view until all that has to be said about it has been said. But the object, if it were actually before us, would continue to assert itself in a thousand ways, and its persistency—its refusal, as it were, to believe that it can be monotonous to us—is its reality, and if its reality, then surely its poetry also.

> You have waited, you always wait, you dumb, beautiful
> ministers,
> We receive you with free sense at last, and are insatiate
> henceforward.

Why should not words imitate things and keep up the same patient knocking at the mind's doors until we genuinely admit them?

The meaning of repetition lies of course in the fact that it is impossible to have the same experience twice. If there is to be value in the repeating over and over of some form of words, there must be something in them or in their varying contexts to enable the mind to pass from a first to a second impression of them, and from a second to a third and a fourth, feeling at each stage that more is added in discovery than is lost through the trouble of treading the old path. Words, we must recollect, are partly vehicles of truth, partly vehicles of emotion; they may exhibit a simple relation or suggest a complex one. Now the more complex the relation suggested, the more familiar we must be with the words that suggest it if we are to profit by every breath of suggestion they contain. We have only to grasp the sense of a geometrical proposition and we have done with the words of it; we have no disposition to say them over. But the words of a poem we often learn by heart and repeat them to ourselves as we might repeat a prayer. We are conscious that they proceed out of a certain state of feeling which we desire to enter into and to make our own; to enter into a state we must become familiar with it as an experience; and so we repeat the poem over and over to ourselves, at each repetition experiencing more intimately and more profoundly the spiritual state reflected in it. The poem thus becomes less and less a form of words to us and more and more a key to life. The reason is that the disposition of the words demands from the mind that is to understand them a corresponding disposition. They emanate from and represent a harmony into which we enter only by reproducing it in our own being.

What applies to our deliberate repetition of a poem to ourselves can be applied to the handling of a poem by its composer if he so chooses. His object is not to state truths but to convey feelings; and the feeling with which we hear a certain form of words may well depend precisely upon the fact that we are not hearing it for the first time, the feeling itself changing and developing as its occasion is repeated. Lyric poetry acknowledges the virtue of repetition in the refrain, which, though in the main a concession to the forms of the musical accompaniment, has its value in reviving and sustaining the implied emotional mood.

But there is a further point. A truth necessarily continues true. Of an emotion our chief test is the degree to which it admits of constancy; feelings are habitually proved and established by a frequent reiteration of the expression of them. Now poetry gives us this assurance as a rule by the elevation of manner, the unified tone, the remoteness, which are in themselves evidences of sustained feeling, being unattainable without it. Repetition (with certain exceptions irrelevant here) is thus more otiose in poetry than in prose. For the web of expression is more tightly woven, every word has full force, and a higher concentration is demanded of the reader who is to assimilate the mood. The poem does not so much rise to a certain altitude, as exist there; and the danger is not that we may doubt the emotion, but that we may fail to recognise the objects to which it attaches—a failing which sometimes extends beyond a poet's readers to the poet himself.

Now the absence of recognised formalities which is characteristic of *Leaves of Grass* robs language of these high-pitched associations, and obliges us to interpret it in accordance with the dictates of mere common sense. When Whitman bids us

> Behold this compost, behold it well,

we know that if we take up a handful of garden soil and turn it over in our hands, we shall be quite in the spirit of his intention. It was one of his ideals in poetry not to lose sight of these everyday simplicities. Yet a form or style which begins from and reverts to such simplicities must forge instruments of some kind to carry it from the simplicities to the profundities. Poetic exaltation is not the less necessary because it is not presupposed. And of Whitman's instruments for obtaining it, repetition—repetition of forms, of phrases, of themes—is perhaps the chief. It is not only that it assists him, as we have seen, to carry out the principle of accumulating weight, his first law of construction. It is also that by it he brings home to us the increasing value for emotion of expressions the value of which, at first hearing, seemed to lie in their very divorce from it, in their cool substantiality. His most astonishing effects are thus often produced by means least compatible with ordinary poetry, the means, like the effects they serve, being peculiarly his own. *Crossing Brooklyn Ferry* is perhaps the greatest and boldest example of them :—

Flood-tide below me ! I see you face to face !
Clouds of the west—sun there half an hour high—I see you also face to face !

Beginning thus with the common attitude to common objects, we find ourselves gradually, as it were, intermingled with them and caught up through the medium of the poet's interpretation into the sentiment and atmosphere they create :—

Ah ! what can ever be more stately and admirable to me than mast-hemm'd Manhattan ?
River and sunset and scallop-edg'd waves of flood-tide ?

Without losing touch with our own experience, we make a passage from natural to impassioned vision. We do more than read poetry. We feel it in its process and formation ; not lifted into another world, but acquainted with the deepening and extending vistas of the world we live in :—

Flow on, river ! flow with the flood-tide, and ebb with the ebb-tide !
Frolic on, crested and scallop-edg'd waves !
Gorgeous clouds of the sunset ! drench with your splendor me, or the men and women generations after me !
Cross from shore to shore, countless crowds of passengers !
Stand up, tall masts of Mannahatta ! stand up, beautiful hills of Brooklyn ! . . .
You have waited, you always wait, you dumb, beautiful ministers,
We receive you with free sense at last, and are insatiate henceforward,
Not you any more shall be able to foil us, or withhold yourselves from us,
We use you, and do not cast you aside—we plant you permanently within us,
We fathom you not—we love you—there is perfection in you also,
You furnish your parts toward eternity,
Great or small, you furnish your parts toward the soul.

There is in this a living presentment of the condition out of which all poetry springs. It is sometimes made a criticism of Whitman that, instead of writing poetry, he writes about it and tries to explain what it is. Often he does so; but often when he seems to be doing so, he is in reality doing much more. He is communicating not merely a poem, an example of poetry, but the spiritual attitude, which if we can assimilate it, will make us according to our measure poets ourselves. No process of explanation serves here. It is work for the greatest of poets in their moments of greatest inspiration. *Crossing Brooklyn Ferry* is such a 'poem of poetry'; it summarises experience, offers a new key to that dark door, would endow us with a new experiencing faculty. A purpose so sublime may well have demanded this strange blend of the ecstasies of music, the exactitudes of speech.

It will be pertinent to observe, finally, that Whitman has discovered and elaborated in *Leaves of Grass* a form for which other poets seem to have searched in vain. What after all was Goethe seeking for in those splendid lyrics *Prometheus, Ganymed* and their like, if not some principle of equivalence for his lines which would be independent of metrical ties or would at least enable him to override them? Such a lyric as *Prometheus* has of course a sustained exaltation of manner, a conciseness of symbolic allusion, which Whitman never aims at and which, even if he had aimed at it, he probably could not have compassed. But considering it on its formal side only, may we not attribute to the lack of Whitman's 'substantial equivalence' that element of trickery or experimentation which the lines seem so often to display? The poet halts, as it were, between two principles, only half conscious of their antagonism, with the result that justice is done to neither:—

Ihr nähret kummerlich
Von Opfersteuern
Und Gebetshauch
Eure Majestät,
Und darbtet, wären
Nicht Kinder und Bettler
Hoffnungsvoller Thoren.

Irony towers here, and it is piled up on something like the substantial principle, until at the word 'wären' the spell is broken, and we revert to measurement by syllables. The next stanza:—

Da ich ein Kind war,
Nicht wusste wo aus noch ein,
Kehrt' ich mein verirrtes Auge
Zur Sonne, als wenn drüber wär'
Ein Ohr, zu hören meine Klage,
Ein Herz, wie mein's,
Sich des Bedrängten zu erbarmen.—

exhibits precisely those faults of which Whitman was sensitive in his first drafts for *Leaves of Grass.* The actual line division is not the real one. There is an inherent discrepancy between the style and the form. Exactly the same defect appears in the English imitations of Goethe to which Matthew Arnold was so much addicted. Some of his best thought is to be found in work which he has thrown into this irregular recitative ; but the poetic result is, by general admission, unsatisfactory. Sometimes his themes are Whitmanesque :—

> They see the Scythian
> On the wide steppe, unharnessing
> His wheel'd house at noon.
> He tethers his beast down, and makes his meal,
> Mare's milk, and bread
> Baked on the embers : all around . . .

Such a passage as this fails, again, precisely for lack of any determining principle in the lines, anything to assure us that, in the absence of metrical regularity, they do not simply begin and end at haphazard. Mere variableness is not only unpleasing but unintelligible. In order that change should have a meaning, we must have with it an instrument for measuring it, a standard to which it may be applied. Whitman makes an original contribution to poetic craft in that he discovers and exhibits a new standard, a new basis for variation. The freedom of his lines is pleasurable to us and conveys an intelligible impression only in so far as we instinctively recognise the common principle they exemplify, and measure them by tacit reference to it.

IV

THE FORM (iii)
THE QUESTION OF UNITY

Of all Whitman's claims on behalf of *Leaves of Grass*, none seems more whimsical, none is harder to accept, than that which would erect the whole book into an artistic unity. Yet the analysis of his form which has been given in the last two chapters will not have been justified unless it induces the reader to accept this final proposition with some seriousness. So long as eulogy of the work is confined to a more or less vague rapture, associated with the idea that form is transcended in it, the statement that the poems constitute an organic whole may be taken to mean no more than that, since they are formless, there is nothing to prevent any number of them from adhering together and, finally, from being bound up in a book to every page of which we recognise one author's name as equally appropriate. But just in so far as we can trace in the parts the workings of a spirit of shaping imagination, we shall be prepared to admit the possibility of some more vital cohesion in the work as a whole.

What is the test of artistic unity in a work? *Leaves of Grass* clearly exceeds altogether the span of human attention. It could not be assimilated at a sitting even by a reader who had preparatorily acquainted himself with every page in detail. Or even supposing that there exists somewhere the giant appetite which could thus absorb and experience the work in its totality, it is not in reference to abnormal power of this kind that we should call it one. Literature of course abounds with works which are recognisably coherent without being readable at a stretch. It is no more necessary to a work that the experience of it should be unbroken when it is read than when it is written. To compose a work of art may be the business of a lifetime, and it may also conceivably take a lifetime to assimilate it: to arrive, by repeated fragmentary readings and re-readings, at the point of view from which the work emanated. The question is not how long it takes the average man to arrive at a comprehensive view of the work, but whether the work is inherently comprehensible at all, whether all its parts do contribute anything appreciable to one another or are dependent for any portion of their meaning upon their relation to one another and to the whole: not whether we can experience it continuously, but whether the experience, when we get it, has continuity, is a continuous experience.

Such a word as "comprehensible" is, of course, inadequate to the situation. There is nothing to prevent a number of works of art from being put before us one after another in such a way that we can see meaning in the arrangement of them and recognise that they set one another off, while yet we can find no inherent affinity in them and nothing but what is accidental and external in their relation to one another. Their relation will in this case be comprehensible and will appeal to a different faculty from that to which they make their separate appeal as works of art. If a number of works are to form a unity together, it is necessary that there should be in each of them some quality which all the others reinforce, not merely in the sense that they explain but rather in the sense that they fulfil one another, so that each has in it, as it were, some seed which the rest exhibit in its germination, in the varying stages of its growth or in its full development. The unity of a work of art is in fact that most composite and concrete of phenomena, an emotional unity, and its parts are only true parts when they have a different effect upon the reader who feels them as parts only and upon the reader who feels them as emanating from the spirit of which the whole is the explicit revelation.

Leaves of Grass, when we first open it, affects us as a volume of quotations, where occasional oases are embedded in long stretches of desert territory, a scrapbook most pages of which we hurriedly turn over, merely allowing our eyes to alight here and there in admiration of some item or group of items. The number of readers who have passed beyond this stage of unfamiliarity is, I suppose, few. For the qualities in the book which repay close attention do nothing to provoke it, lying hid until it is given. Superficial appearances all point to the completest detachment and disconnectedness in the parts. A book of lyrics has at least so much unity that it gives you a succession of pieces all executed at a recognisable emotional level. But in this, while certain obvious emotions appear in-woven in the fabric or stand out in spots of colour, the general effect is that of a common patchwork quilt, made up of fragments out of the rag-bag. Nevertheless, the student of Milton who reads one book of *Paradise Lost* is in a better position to gauge the value and significance of the whole poem than the student of Whitman who judges him by chosen morsels—even though the choice be well and wisely made.

To admit an apparent chaos is to claim that the unity of the work if it exists is elusive and profound. The connecting principle, the constructive motive, must be of sufficient subtlety to interfuse itself with these jarring and conflicting elements, to find its expression equally in all the diverse currents that meet and contend at the surface. It must be " large and contain multitudes." It must be a circumambient atmosphere. Let us note at once then that to provide such an atmosphere was Whitman's conscious aim from the beginning. His *Song of Myself* was not put forth as a completed work, but as the first word of a body of poetic composition which, he confidently announced, was to be his chosen occupation through life. And hardly has he made his bow and introduced himself, before he lays down a distinction between " perfumes," the more or less artificial and specialised flavour of the products of literary art, and the effluence which his own work is to breathe forth :—

> Houses and rooms are full of perfumes, the shelves are crowded with perfumes,
> I breathe the fragrance myself and know it and like it,
> The distillation would intoxicate me also, but I shall not let it.

The atmosphere is not a perfume, it has no taste of the distillation, it is odorless,
It is for my mouth forever, I am in love with it,
I will go to the bank by the wood and become undisguised and naked,
I am mad for it to be in contact with me.

or again, making use of the metaphor which gave his work its name :—

This is the grass that grows wherever the land is and the water is,
This is the common air that bathes the globe.

To aim at providing such an atmosphere, to be personally in love with it even, does not necessarily imply power to write a book which will enable others to breathe it in. And yet the unity which Whitman set out to attain and which, when he viewed his work in retrospect, he claimed to have expressed in it, can scarcely be better indicated than in these metaphors of his own first choice. The extraordinary patience he displays, his willingness to appear trite, foolish, extravagant, crude, monotonous, indecent, are really the measure of the largeness of his design, of his consciousness of the space to be filled, of the scale and system required of him in the balance, the compensations, the proportion of his work. Thus what seems inartistic in his craftsmanship is often in fact the very sign of his artistic perception and of his faithfulness to his vision; for the appearance of artistry is precisely what would have destroyed the real flavour of his art.

The more intimate our knowledge of *Leaves of Grass* becomes, and the more we apprehend the mutual relations of the parts and feel the spirit and purpose underlying them, the more we find that in every page and by means of the unlikeliest passages, phrases and words, that spirit and purpose are actually conveyed. Poems which had no significance when we first read them, betray a delicate appropriateness and become endeared, if for no other reason, because of the contentment with which they occupy their subsidiary place in the design. In fact, it is borne in upon us that a sustained exaltation pervades the work, and that the large tolerance and hospitality characteristic of it are not so much evidence of undiscriminating taste as of undeviating courage and determination.

Of course the claim we are now making for Whitman cannot be finally substantiated at less cost than that of an open-minded study of *Leaves of Grass* in the light of it. But we can point to a few signs, offer a few suggestions which may be in their degree corroborative.

First we may name a mysterious quality attaching to Whitman's perhaps unexampled power of emotional appeal. He has of course written poems—poems such as *Out of the Cradle* or that less famous but hardly less sublime and tender piece beginning:—

> On the beach at night
> Stands a child with her father—

which are so overpowering in their immediately recognisable beauty, that no mystery attaches to the effect they produce upon us. But, apart from these, there are many passages in *Leaves of Grass* which, read with their context, affect us deeply, and which yet, if we attempt to come to close quarters with them as if to force them to yield up the secret of their power, seem to dissolve away under our hands. A curious point is that this almost irresistible pathos frequently attaches to words which betray, of themselves, no emotional content whatsoever. Such a line as

> Lo, 'tis autumn,

some easy phrase like

> Cool blew the moderate night-wind,

sometimes even those strange solecisms which at first we deride, the "omnes, omnes," or "allons," or "mélange mine own," or "the

Great Camerado, the lover true for whom I pine," these and their like, when their associations collect about them, are capable of bringing us to the verge of tears. I do not suggest that two readers equally familiar with *Leaves of Grass* would find their feelings touched in this mysterious way by the same passages. I suspect rather that the appeal of the work is floating and suffused, and that what happens is that feelings derived from larger contact with it concentrate themselves more or less arbitrarily upon a word here and a phrase there, so that these come to act as symbols and reminders of an elusive virtue which binds the whole together.

Another sign is Whitman's undeniable faculty for the perception and presentment of what we must here call subsidiary atmospheres. It would be absurd to claim for a poet that he had felt and expressed the atmosphere that bathes the world, the atmosphere of universal reconciliation, unless we could show that he was alive to the distinguishing atmospheres of things, their peculiar colour and flavour, their contribution to the white light in which they merge. Our difficulty here will be, as before, the substantiation of what we have to say. On the subject of atmosphere it is easier to be graceful than to be cogent, and quotation generally removes the very quality which it is proposed to exemplify. No one questions Whitman's power of creating an object in a phrase, and in so far as this power depends upon that fuller vision of the object which implies awareness of its atmosphere, our point is won. But had he the faculty of communicating this sort of vision on a larger scale ? The reader who doubts this should turn to such a poem as *To a Locomotive in Winter*, withdrawing attention from the splendid climax,

> Fierce-throated beauty !

and observing the successive touches of description and their effect as a series, some of them as bold in their meticulous conscientiousness as others in their impressionistic freedom. The meticulousnesses—such seemingly crude interpolations as

> Thy ponderous side-bars, parallel and connecting rods,—

may appear to be destructive of atmosphere. The effect of them perhaps belongs to the larger composition of which the study of the engine is a detail. Yet the engine itself remains clothed in appropriate poetry ; with its 'twinkling wheels,' its 'train of cars merrily following,' it has been 'merged in verse.'

A scene of public rejoicing, if only because its obvious flavours impose themselves and have to be transcended, is a more exacting subject. This is how Whitman expresses it :—

When million-footed Manhattan unpent descends to her pavements,
When the thunder-cracking guns arouse me with the proud roar I love,
When the round-mouth'd guns out of the smoke and smell I love spit their salutes,
When the fire-flashing guns have fully alerted me, and heaven-clouds canopy my city with a delicate thin haze . . .

The last line has one of those delicious inconsequences which only poetry can afford, and upon which only masters of their medium can venture. From the roar of the cannonade, " alerted " by it, we pass to the vapour idly adrift above our heads, and, born of this opposition of silence and clangor—as though a link had been found between its gorgeous palaces and the cloud-phantasms into which they must dissolve—the whole city rises before us, bathed in light, a beautiful apparition.

Of course, the strength of Whitman's handling in this respect comes out notably in his treatment of those topics which are, so to speak, all atmosphere. The section of *Leaves of Grass* entitled *Sea-Drift* contains the sea, as nothing else in literature contains it, "leaves of salt lettuce," "scales from shining rocks," "weeds and the sea-gluten," and the ocean-waves "reproachfully rolling sands and drift, knowing not why." Whitman too is without an equal when he touches upon all those great amplitudes of nature, of which the sea is but one—

> The large unconscious scenery of my native land,

the night and stars, sunrise, noon, sunset, the "rolling earth." To say that he impersonates these things would be to introduce into his treatment precisely that touch of unreality which he is great enough to have dispensed with. The more we consider the point, the more *Leaves of Grass* appears before us as essentially a study of atmospheres, the atmosphere of youth and aggressiveness in the *Song of Myself* and other early pieces, the atmosphere of maturity and equipoise in the main bulk of the work, and finally the atmosphere of old age and contentment, the "ineffable grace of dying days." Nor does death balk him. Viewing it as he does not in its effects but in its essence, it does not pass for him into a mere natural fact, it remains a theme for poetry.

> Give me your tone, O Death, that I may accord with it,

is his strange apostrophe, and all night the sea whispers to him and " very plainly before daybreak " the " low and delicious word "

> Death, death, death, death, death.

A vision of death " serenely arriving, arriving," a vision which passes beyond death the accident or catastrophe and indifferent goal to find in it the implication and fulfilment of life, is really formulated and held in *Leaves of Grass*. And here, so far as Whitman convinces us, he can convince by nothing but by the atmosphere with which his words are endowed and through which they thus succeed in evoking illumination in a region of mystery. Is he merely throwing, over a subject to which it is inapplicable, the veil of an unreflective optimism, or has he really discerned something specific and significant ? It is a question of atmosphere; and to judge of it securely the reader must study his work in its larger conformation. His decision as to whether Whitman has effectively seized and expressed the " tone of death," and his feeling as to the final unity of *Leaves of Grass* as a work of art, will be interdependent. For the quality of the atmosphere enveloping the whole lies precisely in its balance of positive and negative ingredients, in its exhaustive claim for life and its calm perception of life as a means and an instrument, in its equal assertion of the known life and the unknown, and its final reference of all experiences to the experiencing soul.

The blab of the pave, tires of carts, sluff of boot-soles,
    talk of the promenaders,
The heavy omnibus, the driver with his interrogating
    thumb, the clank of the shod horses on the granite
    floor,
The snow-sleighs, clinking, shouted jokes, pelts of snow-
    balls,
The hurrahs for popular favourites, the fury of rous'd
    mobs . . .
I mind them or the show or resonance of them—I come
    and I depart.

The import of this haphazard envisagement of concrete things is in their power of ballast. For the more a man shows us that he has seen what we see, the more we can believe him when he professes a new vision. So it is that a passage like that just quoted is balanced and explained, to a poetical perception, in a poem like this :—

Whispers of heavenly death murmur'd I hear,
Labial gossip of night, sibilant chorals,
Footsteps gently ascending, mystical breezes wafted
    soft and low,
Ripples of unseen rivers, tides of a current flowing, for-
    ever flowing,
(Or is it the plashing of tears ? the measureless waters of
    human tears ?)

I see, just see skyward, great cloud-masses,
Mournfully slowly they roll, silently swelling and mixing,
With at times a half-dimm'd sadden'd far-off star,
Appearing and disappearing.

(Some parturition rather, some solemn immortal birth ;
On the frontiers to eyes impenetrable,
Some soul is passing over.)

Shall we praise here the exquisite observation, raised in the second stanza to an almost unimaginable beauty, or the exquisite suggestiveness, to which every word in the first stanza seems to make its individual contribution ? Or shall we not rather praise the perfect fusion of the two, the mind so keyed that the clouds move for it and the winds blow with spiritual dignity, while the soul, enlarged, becomes worthy of the sublimest aspects of its dwelling-place ?

V

STYLE

I hear you whispering there O stars of heaven,
O suns—O grass of graves—O perpetual transfers and promotions,
If you do not say any thing how can I say any thing?

. . . . The poet is the equable man . . .
He judges not as the judge judges but as the sun falling round a helpless thing.

In the handling of style as of form Whitman set out with clearly marked intentions. The nicety with which he considered every problem incidental to his work appears in such details as his avoidance of English place names (even his native New York is always Manhattan in his poetry) and his preference for the bare Fourth-month, Fifth-month, etc. of Quaker phraseology over April, May and the rest, with their aroma of literary and historical associations. Among his earliest notes and jottings, now published by his executors, we find " Make no quotations and no reference to any other writers ": " It seems to me to avoid all poetical similes—to be faithful to the perfect likelihoods of nature—healthy, exact, simple, disclaiming ornaments." These seemingly artificial deprivations had their positive sanction; they were to prepare the way for a poetry "hasting, urging, resistless, . . . florid, spiritual," for "the Strength, Command and Luxuriance of Oratory," for "a new burial service" (with the past for corpse) "a book of new things." "Lumber the writing with nothing—let it go as lightly as a bird flies in the air or a fish swims in the sea"; this is the central idea of all.

We have seen that Whitman aimed at transcending form as form is commonly understood; he endeavoured also, more quixotically and not less resolutely, to transcend language, to emancipate the mind from the bondage of accepted symbols.

> Were you thinking that those were the words, those upright lines? those curves, angles, dots?
> No, those are not the words, the substantial words are in the ground and sea,
> They are in the air, they are in you. . . .

> The truths of the earth continually wait, they are not so conceal'd either,
> They are calm, subtle, untransmissible by print,
> They are imbued through all things conveying themselves willingly.

A poet seldom starts out with a formulated perception and acknowledgment of the limitations of his instrument. He tends to regard poetry as the vindication of the power of words, the proof of the limitlessness of their appeal. But Whitman insists that language is a close system, a web of artifices, and that the highest use of it is that which will never allow the medium of interpretation to usurp the place of the thing to be interpreted.

I swear I begin to see little or nothing in audible words,
All merges toward the presentation of the unspoken meanings of the earth . . .

The strange verb to " tally," the strange substantive " rapport " are words which he uses familiarly, as a kind of *leit motiv* running all through *Leaves of Grass*, to keep these ideas in view. He feels that the mind, in its efforts to subdue and understand the world, sets up arbitrary boundaries, is imprisoned in figments and condemned to the company of the skeleton survivals of its own past. Language itself becomes a crystallisation of dead memories instead of a highway to truth. Truth requires us to retain a sense of undiscovered margins, to keep the perceived in relation to the unperceived, to hold open the doors of possibility, to prevent achievement from casting its shadow before it and blocking out our vision of a developing future.

This is often concealed from us by the fact that the use of words is largely a matter of practice or inherited faculty. The child-prodigy sits at the piano and interprets Beethoven without grasping the significance of the experience he records. Other prodigies similarly work wonders with chords and arpeggios played upon the instrument of speech, words being the centre and pivot of their consciousness, a suggestion of experience, even a substitute for experience, instead of a derivation from it. In the din and confusion of the multitude of words written and spoken, we forget wherein the value and meaning of language lies.

O what is it in me that makes me tremble so at voices ?
Surely whoever speaks to me in the right voice, him or her I shall follow,
As the water follows the moon, silently, with fluid steps, anywhere around the globe . . .
For only at last after many years, after chastity, friendship, procreation, prudence, and nakedness,
After treading ground and breasting river and lake,
After a loosen'd throat, after absorbing eras, temperaments, races, after knowledge, freedom, crimes,
After complete faith, after clarifyings, elevations, and removing obstructions,
After these and more, it is just possible there comes to a man, a woman, the divine power to speak words.

To put it otherwise, the art of language at its highest, the art of poetry, exists to acquaint us through words with the larger poetry of life itself. True poetry is not a distillation, a fortified essence, from which the impurities of the world have been driven off and its dregs purged away. It is a shadow, an indirection, a faint reflex. It is an abstraction; and its function is to refer us to the concrete and transcendent reality from which it has been derived. The living, 'real' poem has the same organic harmonies as its derivative, and adds to them the qualities of action, solidity, development. It is not a composition but a personality. It is man himself, with the world he conquers, the world he inaugurates.

Poetry is thus for Whitman the sought, the unfound; for there is only one perfect poem possible, the living universe. Every individual repeats that poem as best he can in the terms which his own life provides; every vessel of consciousness is in potential relation with the whole. In proportion as these potentialities are realised, the individual becomes a more and more responsive medium for the translation of them and, if he have the gift of words, may be impelled to write. But the essence of what he writes is and must be its implicit reference to the one, the only, poem, its reception and radiation of divine light. Whitman founds all upon this implicit essence, making it a constant theme and an acknowledged stimulus in the treatment of lesser themes. It is as if in him the spirit of poetry, returning upon itself, attains self-consciousness.

His domain, as a result of this attitude, grows uncontrollably.

> Tout bonheur que la main n'atteint pas n'est qu'un rève

was the doctrine of the well-moderated Frenchman; and Blake, from a different point of view, represents the universe as being for each man his plot of ground with the sun and stars that rise and shine upon him. Whitman, with all the stress he lays upon the futility of any substitute for experience, cannot tolerate the thought of limitations. The joy of life, the food of poetry, lies for him in its declared relation to the sum of all things. The implicit must become explicit. His poetry is his desire for poetry, his method a method of continuous expansion. His object as a writer is to exhibit the universe in samples, with a hint that every sample is an index of the quality of all the wares: to present, at one and the same time, the distinctness of the details of experience and their fluidity, the sharp contrasts and the unfailing reconciliation.

The key to an understanding of the style of *Leaves of Grass* is the perception that, while a deep intuition dictated the poet's aim, his tactics were as a rule primitive, owing their success, when they succeeded, to the sustaining virtue of the intuition. The tactics, though primitive, were reactionary and in that sense sophisticated; and it is as well to recognise that the blending in him of the reactionary and the primitive was Whitman's salvation. On other terms he would have had no choice but to be dumb. The circumstances of his life were such that he could not have learned the full technique of poetry and retained his natural plastic genius; he could not have mastered completely both the art of literary expression and the self it was his mission to express. His bluntness and aggressive self-confidence were protective traits but for which his creative impulse must have been diverted or checked. Art is long, life is short, and there is a point at which the burden of traditions and accomplishments becomes unbearable. The stores of poetry accumulated in the literature and experience of his race were to Whitman an encumbrance. He felt it necessary to begin again from the beginning.

He felt it necessary; he did not find it possible. When a development has occurred, a man may fall in with it and do his part in carrying it forward, or he may resist it and kick against the pricks. The one thing from which he is debarred is the being or behaving as if there had been no development. Whitman's poetry was intended for simple persons ; but though blunt, it is not simple. Simple poetry is poetry that sings and rhymes ; and hand in hand with these amenities goes the coloured language appropriate to the emotions out of which they spring. Conversational poetry, however rapturous, is as unpleasing to the popular mind as the formalities of verse would be in conversation. Whitman postulates in us the habits and preconceptions against which he is protesting. His is a literary effort, and its literariness is its " burial " of the past, its attempt to shake free from tradition.

His love of the catalogue is a case in point. If a man walks on four feet like an animal, his action derives heightened significance from the fact that, other men walking on two and expecting him to do the same, they examine the cause of his idiosyncrasy. If a poet discards all the accepted associations of his art, he gains for his work at least the prominence of peculiarity, with a direct appeal to the emotion of wonder. Whitman's writing is deliberately exceptional. He is sustained in his work by the pleasure it gives him to be unlike everybody else. To feel and resist the pressure of convention is one of his characteristic joys. The catalogue owes its place in his poetic structure to the fact that it is the last thing the reader would expect to find there. Here, extended before us, is a calculated violation of all canons, a piece of writing the effect of which is to turn all other writing upside-down. But it would have been insolent and useless to shock our minds in this way, unless, the shock applied, new themes and meanings, a new power of perception, were to be opened up to us. The irresponsible reader skips Whitman's catalogues; the critic cannot afford to imitate him. Even here he can maintain that the positive side of the performance, if not the most prominent, is at least the most important and the most vital.

The objections to specification as a literary method are so obvious that we need not rehearse them. Whitman, whatever his faults, is under no misconception as to the principles on which his lists are made or the effect they are likely to have upon a reader. "O lands," he writes, summarising that strangest and most courageous of all his chants, *Our Old Feuillage*,

O lands! all so dear to me—what you are (whatever it is),
I putting it at random in these songs, become a part of that, whatever it is,

and later

> Singing the song of these my ever-united lands . . .
> . . . these me,
> These affording in all their particulars the old feuillage to me and to America, how can I do less than pass the clew of them, to afford the like to you ?

" I putting it at random in these songs, whatever it is," " how can I do less ? " the claim is so moderate and so candid that only arrogance could refuse to hear it out. The point to Whitman is that the multiplicity, the inexhaustibility of things must somehow be reflected in poetry, unless, indeed, the bonds of truth and beauty are to be severed. He sets out to bring before us the many-faceted realities of the world, and the initial poetic fact to him is plenty. The philosopher might quarrel with us were we to say that, if being is good, more being is better. But to Whitman a leaf or a butterfly is embodied perfection, and two leaves or two butterflies, though not more perfect than one, embody twice as much perfection and are twice as much to be desired. Spaciousness, fertility, and even the redundance of the vital processes were inspiration to him, and he would gladly have counted the drops of water in the sea and the stars in the sky. He is a beginner in poetry, but there is this of the master in him, that he begins with delight.

> Beginning my studies the first step pleas'd me so much,
> The mere fact consciousness, these forms, the power of motion,
> The least insect or animal, the senses, eyesight, love,
> The first step I say awed me and pleas'd me so much,
> I have hardly gone and hardly wish'd to go any farther,
> But stop and loiter all the time to sing it in ecstatic songs.

Thus he brings as first positive quality to his lists an insatiable love of detail and the artist's instinctive conviction that his pleasure will be communicated. They are sadly abbreviated examples of the lists he would like to have drawn up. To this abbreviating emotion—these lines left out—they owe their charm.

Yet it is the essence of a list that it should contain not only what is interesting but also what is uninteresting. Few would say that Whitman's were disqualified in this respect; and perhaps the general impression would be that he has wantonly choked them with mere items. If the whole hulk does not sink into oblivion, is it not, readers will urge, because some detail is here and there made vivid, and that these vivid details, like water-tight compartments, buoy it up? Take, for example, such a passage as the following :—

You whoever you are !
You daughter or son of England !
You of the mighty Slavic tribes and empires ! you Russ in Russia !
You dim-descended, black, divine-soul'd African, large, fine-headed, nobly-form'd, superbly destin'd, on equal terms with me !
You Norwegian ! Swede ! Dane ! Icelander ! you Prussian !
You Spaniard of Spain ! you Portuguese !
You Frenchwoman and Frenchman of France ! etc. etc.

The absurdities and anomalies of this are plain. Is it pretended that the order of mention, the relative prominence given to one name or another, are more than accidental ? Is there sense or reason in saying " Spaniard of Spain " and in not saying " Norwegian of Norway " : in mentioning the Frenchwoman and not the Spanishwoman ; in suggesting that there are Frenchmen and Spaniards who do not belong to France and Spain, or that if there are, they are to be excluded ? Such objections have a certain irrelevance and inconclusiveness. The claim they would dispose of is a claim that Whitman does not advance. His shifting styles of nomenclature, the trifling illogicalities of his enumeration, are merely formal. His hope is that they will keep our attention alert enough to accept, not indeed every item of the list, but the list itself and the fact that it has been held worth making, as something solid, something to be reckoned with. It is as if we were required to walk through a gallery of pictures, with a guide whose object it was to show us not the pictures but the picture-gallery; and that to this end we must both walk through the building and walk out of it. Whitman is not content until he has brought us out finally into the open. When he has us there, he does not pretend that we have seen the pictures. We have glimpsed at them; we know that they are there. He does not mention all the tribes of the earth in his inventory; yet he hopes to convince us that for a certain purpose he has virtually brought them forward every one. "They are all in the dictionary." Yes; but they are in the dictionary for a different reason. Here they are mentioned in order that we may wish them all "Health and Good Will" and understand that

> Each of us is inevitable,
> Each of us limitless—each of us with his or her right
> upon the earth,
> Each of us allow'd the eternal purports of the earth,
> Each of us here as divinely as any of us is here.

The purpose of the list, with its haphazard items, is to form our minds to this universal receptiveness, to give concreteness to our idea of universality and to our sense of brotherhood. The occasional prominence of a vigorous detail is to assure us further that the more we achieve such an attitude, the more there will be for us of poetry in the world. And the essential point in connection with the stylistic presentment of the whole is, that the vigorous details, but for their occurrence in a list, would absorb our attention to themselves, while, placed as they are, they distribute their vitality, acting not as the air-tight compartment, but as the life-giving lungs. So it is that after

> You Roman! Neapolitan! you Greek!

we have

> You lithe matador in the arena at Seville!
> You mountaineer living lawlessly on the Taurus or Caucasus!
> You Bokh horse-herd watching your mares and stallions feeding!
> You beautiful-bodied Persian at full speed in the saddle shooting arrows to the mark!

and such a line as the last, if it is lungs and reviving oxygen to the others, requires the others as a context and enters into its meaning from the fact that they are there, a body needing breath. These remarks must be applied to Whitman's style in general. For

Leaves of Grass is not, after all, a poor mince pie, food for the Jack Horners of literature. Its vivid phrases lose their real flavour when they are picked out; they owe something even to the clumsinesses and solecisms which we pick out for ridicule. There is organic interaction between the parts.

The catalogues, then, have direct artistic value as an expression of Whitman's delight in the mere fact of being, and on this delight the whole fabric of his style securely reposes. They have their obvious absurdity, but they have no touch of deeper impropriety or irrelevance. They represent, at its extreme, his essential virtue, the quality which makes *Leaves of Grass* the perfect title for his work. For his poems have in a unique degree the attribute of diffused equivalence. The parts are all interchangeable; every key fits every door; every sentence seems to put forward a new instance of the ever present, ever elusive truth. The sentiment throughout is as if, by slowly accumulating perceptions and discoveries, some vast, half-obliterated fresco were being rescued from obscurity, the significance of each detail being that it is a detail and that it is in its place:—

> Out of its little hill faithfully rise the potato's dark green leaves.

There is an exquisite piece of restoration!

Old occult Brahma interminably far back, the tender and
junior Buddha,

there is another! and the supply of touches of this kind is inexhaustible. Taken at random, these two consort together well, and reveal at once affinities we could hardly otherwise have suspected. Viewing Whitman in this light, we may say that it is his achievement to have drawn up, as if in précis form, an inventory of the life of the world.

It is not only in his lists, however, that we can discern his impulse to penetrate the formalities of verbiage and seize and present to us the infinite real. The construction of many of his sentences and paragraphs, his eccentric grammar or absence of grammar, some of the minor predilections and some of the chief architectural principles we find in his work, are traceable to his desire to keep words in subservience and to do justice to the culminating poetry of concrete things. One of his familiar tricks is the contented use of a detached string of present participles:—

We two boys together clinging,
One the other never leaving . . .
Power enjoying, elbows stretching, fingers clutching,
Arm'd and fearless, eating, drinking, sleeping, loving,
No law less than ourselves owning, sailing, soldiering,
thieving, threatening . . .
Fulfilling our foray.

The effect both here and wherever Whitman makes use of it is always ugly, but the grammatical incompleteness is intended to emphasise what to him is the chief fact about this and about every theme : the impossibility of summarising and disposing of it. When we read that

> The boy stood on the burning deck, etc.

what is left upon our minds is that an action took place and is now over and done with. And all logical utterance has more or less the same tendency, expressing only a fraction of what it implies and leading us to forget that it implies anything. Whitman resorts to tricks and artifices in order to remind us of the implications of speech. The participial sentence, with its emphasis upon the unfinished, is one of these tricks. Another is total omission of the verb :—

> Once Paumanok,
> When the lilac scent was in the air and Fifth-month grass was growing,
> Up this seashore in some briars.
> Two feather'd guests from Alabama, two together,
> And their nest, and four light-green eggs spotted with brown.

A finished statement fastens our attention not upon objects but upon some modification they undergo. In this, we have a mere form of introduction. We hear of an island which is to be the scene of a drama, of the persons by whom the drama is to be played. The materials of the action are, as it were, thrown down, and left lying before us in their undefinable solidity. For a parallel we must go to Plato's dialogues, where sophists and philosophers open discussion by gravely admitting the existence of the object to be discussed. ἀρετήν τι καλεῖς; "'There is something, Gorgias, that you call virtue?' 'Yes.'" Yet another expedient is vague disregard of the formal requirements of words, and deliberate modelling of the sentence to suit margins of implication :—

Out of the cradle endlessly rocking,
Out of the mocking-bird's throat, the musical shuttle,
Out of the Ninth-month midnight . . .
From those beginning notes of yearning and love there in
    the mist,
From the thousand responses of my heart never to cease,
From the myriad thence-arous'd words,
From the word stronger and more delicious than any,
From such as now they start the scene revisiting,
As a flock, twittering, rising, or overhead passing,
Borne hither, ere all eludes me, hurriedly,
A man, yet by these tears a little boy again . . .

A passage like this springs from the desire to bring together facts, feelings and associations, so numerous, so diverse, that no normal sentence could accommodate them. Its coherence depends upon equivalences and relations which the niceties of common construction would be too rigid to allow. Yet the habit of violating grammar is to be deprecated; for the rules represent the gathered experience of writers as to how meaning is conveyed. An exception is often expressive just because it is an exception ; and there is no need to object to Whitman's anomalies, taken severally. But a line like

> From such as now they start the scene revisiting

not only violates grammar, but leaves us uncertain what kind of violation has taken place. It is a recurring weakness in Whitman's emancipated constructions that, mingled in with emancipation, there is the fumbling and bungling of imperfect technique. The nine liberties which he takes, meaning to take them, suffer from the tenth which he takes without knowing that he has taken it.

In so far as Whitman is a great stylist, it is not his daring unconventionalities that make him so, though these in themselves are such as to argue greatness of a kind. He is great because, having chosen his method, he takes the consequences of his choice with consummate pliability and responsiveness. He has been reflecting on the uses of language, and has struck out a line of his own for the use of it. In spite of this his writing is free from the taint of theory, has none of the rigidity of conscious rebellion, is not the less easy because he has determined to make it so. He takes no word or phrase as having the weight, meaning or implication he has decided shall attach to it; he does not dictate to language, but faithfully allows it to dictate to him, quite undisturbed by its fluidity, ready to interweave together and present as one the remotest aspects of his theme. The crowning example of his power in this is the song of the mocking-bird in *Out of the Cradle Endlessly Rocking.* The bird, like his poet, counts over the natural objects which surround him, apostrophising the sea, the breakers, the moon, the shore, the stars, the wind. But the items of the list, passing under the spell of personal passion, become as it were the instruments of an orchestra; each plays its individual part in a lyrical symphony, and each is in turn identified with the central motive of the whole.

Soothe! soothe! soothe!
Close on its wave soothes the wave behind,
And again another behind, every one lapping, every one close,
But my love soothes not me, not me.

The bird's note, the motion of the waves, the languorous aspect of the moon, the largest and most evanescent suggestions of love in the forces and forms of nature, its fanciful and accidental illusions in the heart of a little creature, all are blended together in a succession of half-descriptive, half-imitative touches, the whole scene and every actor in it being presented to us indifferently from without and from within. Years before "futurism" was heard or thought of, the core of aspiration in its incoherencies has been felt and rendered. Even love's logic of despair is not left out :—

But soft ! sink low !
Soft ! let me just murmur,
And do you wait a moment you husky-nois'd sea,
For somewhere I believe I heard my mate responding to
me,
So faint, I must be still, be still to listen,
But not altogether still, for then she might not come
immediately to me.

Whitman surmounts all difficulties by ignoring them, by resting in complete security upon his obtained results, at every point perceiving what has been expressed and judging what foundation has been provided for further expression.

Thus while the aim of his style is objectivity, its achievement is impressionism. He gives to his words not solidity but atmosphere; and what is the solidity of words if not their atmosphere? The problem of the writer is that words are not things, that they have laws peculiar to them. To put two things together and to put the names of them together are different operations. The catalogue, with its great haul of tangibilities, here finally declares itself; for the wider the net is thrown, the fainter, the more dream-like are the specimens we bring in. All depends upon the subtlest suggestions and evocations. Did we seem to vaunt our brutal indifference to all artistry? it is only the obvious contrivances that we despise!—

You Caffre, Berber, Soudanese!
You haggard, uncouth, untutor'd Bedowee!
You plague-swarms in Madras, Nankin, Kaubul, Cairo!
You benighted roamer of Amazonia! you Patagonian!
    you Feejee-man!

The whole passage affects one like a charm, so curious-magical are its harmonies. One might compare it to Rossetti:—

Cecily, Gertrude, Magdalen,
    Margaret and Rosalys . . .

but the comparison would only bring out Whitman's superior fibre, and the immense value to his composition, for pure beauty, of its apparent carelessness.

Perhaps what is finally most delightful in Whitman's style is the natural and constant interplay of the two qualities which I have tried to bring into relief, his childlike objectivity and his magical suggestiveness. The objectivity does not pall, because the child is a magician; the suggestiveness is not teasing, because the magician is a child. Throughout a lengthy poem he will perhaps deal purely in suggestions, marshalling his objects for the sake of the hints they may contribute of some remote and fleeting analogy; yet these objects will be as temperately and lovingly handled as if their presence before us were a poem in itself:—

> Well-shaped and stately the Great Eastern swam up my
> bay, she was 600 feet long . . .

or:—

> The sea-gulls oscillating their bodies, the hay-boat in
> the twilight, and the belated lighter . . .

Indeed their presence is a poem. Whitman tells us how he would walk the shore of his beloved Paumanok "thinking the old thought of likenesses" or "seeking types"; but the truth is that he has the secret of that emancipated vision to which all types are transitory things, and dissolve one into another. For the task of the poet is to provide contexts through which glimpses of the universal similitudes will appear; and the less he cleaves to such accidental connections as take his eye, the more a poet is he. The simile, the symbol in Whitman is, what he determined to make it, a presupposition of his artistry—condensed into some seemingly casual epithet or implied in the collocation of a series of plain sentences. Thus he can exhibit the shyest mysteries as coolly as the commonest facts; for the common fact has never lost for him its mystery or its shyness :—

> You objects that call from diffusion my meanings and give them shape ![1]
> You light that wraps me and all things in delicate equable showers !
> I believe you are latent with unseen existences, you are so dear to me !

Was there ever a lovelier incantation !

Hitherto we have dealt principally with the formation and texture of Whitman's style; a still more engrossing theme is its tone and colour. *Leaves of Grass* exhibits from this point of view the merging tints of the spectrum, passing from a deep warm scarlet to a pale transparent blue. The progression presents

[1] This is not the only sentence in *Leaves of Grass* that gives us as it were a poetic foreboding of the metaphysic of M. Bergson ; the fascination for Whitman of the "curious" fact of *time* will occur to every reader.

itself as a progression of experience and character. What higher tribute could be paid to it ? The style is the man ; but man, when he takes pen in hand, is apt to be a creature preoccupied with the concealment or display of secondary accommodations and vanities, so that we have to infer him from his mannerisms. Whitman, when we first read him, seems full of mannerisms. But a closer acquaintance convinces us that these are living characteristics, not literary antics. His one great act of rebellion left him free to be his real self, provided his strength and endurance were equal to the task. They were so, and his writing exhibits to us therefore the natural development of a great personality.

In the *Song of Myself* the note is defiance. The poet, in a rapture of mystical affirmation, glorifies the whole apparatus of human egotism, the evil and the good. The soul steps forth to the sound of the trumpet, claiming the Universe for its freehold, cleaving the air with the rigour and determination of its call. The whole pageant of life passes before us, with shawms and cymbals accompanying. Great things are not too great for the procession, nor small too small. The feature of the style is its blend of aggressiveness and fidelity, of delicacy and magnificence. The heat of the creative impulse is equally divided between the determination to impress and the determination to take all impressions; we cannot distinguish between its malleability and its force. Quotation will not illustrate these qualities; for the proof of them is that they are sustained. There is nothing for it but to read the poem. Its fifty-two pages are surely as varied and as invigorating as anything in literature.

The tremendous buoyancy of this early manner to some extent overreaches itself, involving Whitman in inflated expressions, spasmodic transitions and a want of recognisable architecture. With the further maturing of his power, it was a disadvantage to him that in the *Song of Myself* he had, in a sense, covered all his ground. The dangers attaching to expansion, application and repetition often beset him in the remainder of his work. He frequently explains, instead of presenting, truth and finds the temptation to revive his past self irresistible. But his instrument, when he can disencumber it, has a mellower and soberer sound, and we realise that a new range of experience has been opened up to him. The relation of inner to outer, of the soul to the world, which the *Song of Myself* heralded and claimed, is now the poet's achievement. The world is less a challenge and provocation to him, more an associate, a parable, a persuasion. The first demonstrativeness has served its turn therefore; defiance is put by; the prevailing note is a meditative tenderness; we pass to a more withdrawn, a more penetrative portrayal. Instead of sentences that leap keen as the lightning flash, we have the pulsings and fluctuations of an enveloping aurora, electric messages out of some warm summer night, intimate, brooding and diffused; while in the landscape lit by these soft shimmerings the timider denizens of the mind come forth and hidden affinities are confided:—

As I wend to the shores I know not...
As I inhale the impalpable breezes that set in upon me,
As the ocean so mysterious rolls toward me closer and closer,
I too but signify at the utmost a little wash'd-up drift . . .

You friable shore with trails of debris,
You fish-shaped island, I take what is underfoot,
What is yours is mine my father . . .

Kiss me my father,
Touch me with your lips as I touch those I love,
Breathe to me while I hold you close the secret of the murmuring I envy.

Here poetry is action. The drama which the soul enacts behind closed doors, unwatched it may be by itself even, is played with the seashore for a stage and the sea and the sky for chorus. The style is that in the man which has gone to the subjugation of these vast influences conveying itself to us in the fewest words and the simplest sentences that it can find.

We pass to a further stage when, with a new return of the inner upon the outer life, the focus of action changes and the style becomes a clear transcript, the poetry of which is inseparable from that of the deeds it records.

A sight in camp in the daybreak gray and dim,
As from my tent I emerge so early sleepless,
As slow I walk in the cool fresh air the path near by the hospital tent,
Three forms I see on stretchers lying, brought out there untended lying,
Over each the blanket spread, ample brownish woolen blanket,
Gray and heavy blanket, folding, covering all.

Curious I halt and silent stand,
Then with light fingers I from the face of the nearest the first just lift the blanket ;
Who are you elderly man so gaunt and grim, with well-gray'd hair, and flesh all sunken about the eyes ?
Who are you my dear comrade ?

Then to the second I step—and who are you my child and darling ?
Who are you sweet boy with cheeks yet blooming ?

Then to the third—a face nor child nor old, very calm, as of beautiful yellow-white ivory ;
Young man I think I know you—I think this face is the face of the Christ himself,
Dead and divine and brother of all, and here again he lies.

There is something here which the man that has attained to it cannot leave behind. Little more need be said. Nor need we follow in this chapter the symptoms of effort and uncertainty that fell upon Whitman with his paralysis. Some of his greatest utterances belong to that period of prostration and stand out among the ruins crowned with the harmony and beauty of crumbling walls, unroofed, open to heaven :

With Nature's calm content, with tacit huge delight,

or

All those hearts as of fretted children shall be sooth'd,

or

Love that is pulse of all, the sustenance and the pang.

He carried with him to the last a faculty of trance-like perception which enabled him to throw a gleam of poetry over any and every detail of his experience. We noted fidelity as one of the earliest qualities of his style. As his initiative weakens, fidelity becomes a more and more prominent and precious quality, until finally in the *Annexes*, in *Sands at Seventy* and *Good-bye My Fancy*, fidelity and frailty join hands, and the quality of the poetry is its transparent exactitude, as if a mirror were held up before us by a hand satisfied simply that it should not tremble :—

Soon shall the winter's foil be here ;
Soon shall these icy ligatures unbind and melt—A little while,
And air, soil, wave, suffused shall be in softness, bloom and growth . . .
. . . Thou shalt perceive the simple shows, the delicate miracles of earth,
Dandelions, clover, the emerald grass, the early scents and flowers,
The arbutus under foot, the willow's yellow-green, the blossoming plum and cherry ;
With these the robin, lark and thrush, singing their songs—the flitting blue-bird ;
For such the scenes the annual play brings on.

The contentment which is the charm of these last almost impalpable utterances is our final index of what is greatest in *Leaves of Grass*. Whitman is a writer who has divested himself of encumbrances and distinguished beauty from ornamentation. So, at the end, by his flickering candle, he still sees infinite things, and as more and more is taken, the less and less that remains with him is poetry.

VI

PLAN

The threads that were spun are gathered, the weft crosses the warp, the pattern is systematic.

Leaves of Grass has so little in common with other books whether of prose or poetry that the appreciative reader needs, in a peculiar degree, to derive from the book itself the principles by which to pass judgment upon it. His difficulties are increased by the fact that the work is as uneven as it is strange. The whole—a blend of conscious and unconscious art, of passion and reflection—expresses a constant purpose. But the poet's power of realising this purpose varied immensely at different periods of his life; and being a poor critic of his own writings, he finally arranged them without regard for their poetic value, considering merely in what order the thought of each would be most effective in its contribution to the thought of all. His plan, though it is significant, is in many ways so misleading that, if the quality and range of his achievement have been obscured, the fault lies really at his own door. For his manner underwent changes and developments of an unusually subtle kind. He lost in power as he grew older, he gained in perception; and we could no more spare the later than the earlier work. Yet before we can judge finally of the results he attained, we must have traced in his career as an artist the symptoms of this parallel growth and decline, and we must also have distinguished his activity as a compiler from his activity as a poet.

The general purpose of his book, of course, is that it shall be the deliberate and progressive unfolding of the conscious life of a man who is at once individual and typical; and it is so arranged as to present first the foundations and implications of such a life and to fill in afterwards the various stages of experience and reflection. Obviously certain stages of experience must be enacted before they can receive full literary expression. Only as Whitman grows old can we really hear in his poetry the note of age. Yet the requirements of his scheme were clear to him almost from the beginning, and his concluding poem *So Long* was written at the age of forty. Perhaps he had some apprehension that he might not live to realise and be his book; if so, his apprehension was justified. *Leaves of Grass* is an unfinished work. The latter half of the book is a makeshift. While then its progression is confused by the retrospective patchings of the compiler, it is confused also by the anxious anticipations of the poet.

In order not to press too hard the division between them, it is well to remember that in Whitman there was a more or less persisting reconcilement of these two opposites. It was his intention from the first to write in such a way that his poems should derive light from one another, only making their last essential communication when felt through the atmosphere of the whole book. He was deliberately working at a big mosaic and the fitting together of the pieces, though it may seem a mechanical process and in any case might have been done better, was nevertheless quite in accordance with the spirit of his work. The lapses in perception which it involved were accidental and were brought about by the same failure of power which left the original design of the work unrealised.

His plan as a compiler turns upon a principle of rough equivalence. The cubes of his mosaic are of various sizes, but to enable them to co-operate they are sorted into two groups, large and small, on the understanding that a collection of small cubes is to be equivalent to one large one. In other words, a certain number of important poems stand on their own feet (the reader should consult the List of Contents in *Leaves of Grass*) while the rest fall under subtitles and illustrate some phase of experience in their combination. But it was characteristic of Whitman to consult his printer also and to bear in mind the mechanical exigencies for which the printer stands ; we get therefore four short pieces—*Youth, Day, Old Age, and Night*, *Reversals*, *Transpositions*, *A Paumanok Picture*—intercalated and made to appear more important than they are simply in order to avoid gaps in the page.[1]

These disposed of, the skeleton design of the work becomes apparent. We notice first a well-marked introduction, a beginning, a middle and an end. At the middle, as the crowning experience of maturity, we have *Drum Taps*, and associated with it, *Memories of President Lincoln* (his assassination being to Whitman a symbolic event epitomising the significance of the war), and *By Blue Ontario's Shore* (the expression of the meaning of the war in its bearing upon the democracy and literature of a unified America). After this all is, in theory, autumnal—the ripening of accumulated stores,

[1] See *Leaves of Grass*, pp. 180, 276, 332, 351.

the severance of the fruit from the tree, the farewell of the experiencing soul to those " materials " which have been the instruments of its experience. Before it come the introduction of the book to the reader and of its hero to the world.

The introduction includes *Inscriptions* and one important and noble poem *Starting from Paumanok* which, though written like the concluding piece as early as 1860, expounds the whole purpose of *Leaves of Grass*, sounding together its three harmonising notes of individualism and religion and love. Then, with the *Song of Myself*, the work begins in idea as also it began in fact: a lyric rhapsody of fifty pages' length lets the untamed, magnetic, hungering, responsive personality loose among the various and inexhaustible riches of his native America and bids him see himself and be himself in all. All is for the individual, for the soul. The whole creation is to each man severally as a lover.

Love being Whitman's keynote, an *orgelpunkt* that is to sound all through his poems, the fusion of two beings in one, the mutual self-expression and self-surrender which belong to the love of the sexes, is his image of the relation of the soul to the world. The aim of the processes of life is the development of individuality, of identity, through "materials," that is, through our various contacts with the physical world. The sexual relation is the foundation and so, if you will, the symbol of those contacts. Therefore, as soon as, in the *Song of Myself*, the typical complex personality, the world's lover, has been put upon the stage, *Children of Adam* follows, a series of pieces dedicated specifically to sex; while next to *Children of Adam* comes *Calamus*, complementary to it. Action and expression are love. But there is that without which no action or expression would be possible, and that is love too. When we pray, we endeavour to adjust ourselves newly to the world—as it were, to start our lives afresh; and instinctively, in order to give ourselves more completely to a renewed experience, we withdraw from the world of experience for a time, we shut our eyes. *Calamus* is the celebration of the shut eyes of love, of the love that rises above materials and is the condition of our relation to them.

After *Calamus*, the presuppositions of life having been celebrated, we have a series of constructive songs, Whitman's solidest contribution to the developing and crystallising experience of man. Nor is it by a coincidence that the first and last of these relate him to the world, the earth—the first chiefly to the earth in its diversities, the earth as a treasure-house of history, the theatre of the life of men, the last to the earth as a unified condition of spiritual life, perhaps itself a single spiritual being, " the divine ship sailing the divine sea." Of the remainder, the *Song of the Open Road* proclaims the spirit of progress, the advancing, conquering soul to which nothing is and nothing can be inimical except surrender and accepted routine ; *Crossing Brooklyn Ferry* exposes the spiritual structure and substance of so-called material things, and since it has been said that all experience is love, endeavours to induce a state of mind in which we shall see why this is so and how it can be so ; *The Answerer* shows, again, how poetry is the mating of the soul with materials and the terms on which alone their union can be consummated ; and then *Our Old Feuillage,* lovingly, inimitably, illustrates these qualities in concrete detail for the American citizen.

The central place in the group is given characteristically to *A Song of Joys.* Whitman took pleasure in these small points of suggestion ; the reader will humour him.

So far (we have reached page 148) there has been no poem of importance in the book which does not present Whitman in the fullness of exuberant and conscious power; but discrimination now becomes necessary. The four songs following all relate to typical conditions and activities of American life. The first, *Song of the Broad Axe,* belongs to his first period, but it lacks coherence. Already in Whitman's time the axe had ceased to be an effective symbol of American life, and his contrast between the American axe of freedom and the European axe of the executioner is a conceit. The atmosphere of forced image-making which produced such an absurdity impairs the tone of the poem. The *Song of the Exposition,* dating from 1871 (two years before Whitman's paralysis), introduces a new timbre into the work. No longer "august master of beauty," the poet strains after effect and mouths rhetorically, and this in spite of the fact that his theme is congenial to him: we—America, that is—are to produce poetry to-day and to produce it not by idealising it in the past but by realising that we are ourselves its repository, that it is present in the most homely details of our lives:—

> She's here, install'd amid the kitchen ware.

The *Song of the Redwood Tree* (true 'song of the broad axe' this) represents yet another style, being still later in date and sounding those deliberate retrospective harmonies which are characteristic of almost all Whitman's best work after the war, the work of a man whose mysticism has passed from the stage of rapt seizure to that of experience and calmness. *A Song for Occupations* takes us back once more to his vividest and most assertive manner; but again we find a tang of artificiality and wrongheadedness. Perhaps this came of the pretence or of the effort to attract and appeal to the working classes, as such. Whitman must have felt from the beginning that they would be the last to listen to him.

As we approach the central tableland of the work, it is natural that we should encounter a tendency to fit in more or less arbitrarily pieces that have no very precise bearing upon the general design of the book and are valuable chiefly for their reinforcement in new lights or from new angles of ideas already broached. *Birds of Passage* and *By the Roadside*, which precede *Drum Taps*, *Autumn Rivulets* which comes after it, are groups composed in the main of incidental and illustrative pieces. But Whitman kept the idea of progress steadily in view. The contents of *Birds of Passage* and *By the Roadside* suggest that the climax of the pilgrimage of life is still to be reached, while in *Autumn Rivulets* the process of distillation begins. Yet even there the soul still looks and moves forward, although its earthly life is in the main a retrospect.

Birds of Passage opens significantly with the *Song of the Universal,* the theme of which is so perfectly in Whitman's vein, that although the poem was written in the period of his greatest prostration (1874–5) and is weak in its recurrent use of conventional phrase and rhythm, it attains to greatness. *To You* is but another *Song of the Universal,* perfectly exhibiting however Whitman's unique principles of composition. The whole section aims at clarifying that conception of a developing individual which is the root idea of *Leaves of Grass.* Its title is chosen, of course, to suggest the thought of immortality.

A Broadway Pageant is perhaps placed next because while its theme associates it with the middle section of the work, with the period when the faculties and activities of experience are at fullness and poise, it yet anticipates the war and has no direct bearing of any kind upon *Drum Taps.* The reception in America of the first embassy from an Eastern nation suggests to Whitman that a new stage has been reached in the history of the human spirit.

> The sign is reversing, the orb is enclosed,
> The ring is circled, the journey is done.

He foresees the time when all that the West owes to the East will be made good and when the ideas of progress and fraternity will genuinely unite the world. It was a bold prophecy to have made on provocation seemingly so slight in 1860; who would have supposed that in little more than fifty years Republican government would have been attempted in China?

Sea Drift precedes *Drum Taps* in part because the experiences it records and the poems in which those experiences are recorded belonged in point of fact to Whitman's earlier life; but there is also a symbolic appropriateness in the position assigned to it, since it contains the first explicit celebration in *Leaves of Grass*, not of the idea merely, but of the experience, of death and the mystical associations that cling about it, typified to Whitman's mind peculiarly by the sea. Here, before the individual life is merged in the national, we have personality revealed at its core, in the anguish of bereavement, in the prostration of the soul before the fact of death and the thought of what lies beyond it, in its ignorance of what that beyond may be, in the sense of the insignificance of this proud individual, now at last beaten, humiliated,—him of whose claims and assertiveness and insatiability we had heard so much :—

> Me and mine, loose windrows, little corpses,
> (See, from my dead lips the ooze exuding at last,) . . .

These things (while with them, under them, sounds still the note of confidence and security) it was necessary to explore and express and to relate them to the period of fullest maturity, of conscious manhood. *By the Roadside* is a transitional section merely. After *As I ebb'd with the Ocean of Life*, the way to *Drum Taps* is prepared ; and nowhere more intimately than in *Sea Drift* can we realise how great was the poet whose voice those drums were to overwhelm.

The middle section of the book (pp. 219-276) requires no further exposition ; but a few minor distinctions in style must be alluded to. In *Drum Taps*, for example, pieces such as *First, O Songs for a Prelude*, or *Song of the Banner at Daybreak*, or *A Centenarian's Story*, pieces in which Whitman shows himself kindled, sometimes a little artificially, by the thought of the struggle rather than by the facts of it, are a class apart. There is in these and one or two others a touch of the inflation to which he is subject whenever he is not deeply at home with his theme, and which has sometimes been supposed an essential characteristic of his poetry. Needless to say it is in such pieces as *Vigil Strange* or *A Sight in Camp* that he is himself, and in these there is still the complete formal mastery, which from this time forward, with his broken health, we are less and less able to rely on finding in his work. The assassination of Lincoln gave him a unique opportunity ; but *When Lilacs Last in the Dooryard Bloom'd*, majestic as it is, does not maintain the proud aloofness of rhythm which never forsakes him at his best. Its passages of conventional melody, verging upon sing-song, have no doubt made the dirge more popular than it otherwise could have been; and have led it to be accepted as the very thing they prevent it from being—a type of his work.

By Blue Ontario's Shore is perplexing at first, because though it speaks of the war as past, it is yet written, the bulk of it, in the style of the first period. It was in 1856, of course, that Whitman described himself as one

> who walks the States with a barb'd tongue :—

by 1865 such a description would have been both uncharacteristic and inapplicable. But the demand for America of a national voice, a school of poets, who should bring her ideals home to the minds of the people and fuse them together, seemed to him even more urgent and irresistible after the war than it had done before it; and he therefore recasts this song of poetry and democracy and brings his ideals into relation with the reviving hopefulness of national life after the struggle. The reader has only to compare the parenthesis in section 11,

> Angry cloth I saw there leaping

with the passages on either side of it, to feel at once the kind of weakness into which Whitman's later manner betrays him :—

> I stand again In leaden rain
> Your flapping folds saluting.

Whenever his theme imposes upon him an effort beyond his strength, he succumbs to " prettiness."

In *Autumn Rivulets* mixture of styles becomes rampant, and from this point onward *Leaves of Grass* is a mere mêlée. Most of the ' rivulets ' have an intelligible link with the idea expressed in the introductory poem *As Consequent,* but they lack the subtler and only true artistic connection, the connection of tone and flavour. We said earlier that Whitman's arrangement of his poems followed subject only; the statement was of course too crude. For wherever we have art at all, subject and treatment are indistinguishable, and Whitman is aware that it is not by their obvious labels but by their ultimate suggestions that poems must be classified. It is on this account precisely that our confusion now becomes serious. We are on the look-out for hints and indirections, for meanings dropped by the way; and these hints and meanings too often contradict one another. *Warble for Lilac Time* gives, we may imagine, the note that Whitman would have liked to sound continuously through *Autumn Rivulets*, but even those 'leaves' which are autumnal in date by no means always sound it clearly. *There was a Child Went Forth, This Compost, To a Foil'd European Revolutionnaire, Unnamed Lands, Song of Prudence, Who Learns My Lesson Complete*, are all in Whitman's earliest manner, while there are few of the more incisive pieces in the section that had not appeared already in the edition of 1860. At the period of life which *Autumn Rivulets* theoretically represents, the measure of Whitman's artistic success is the measure of his contentment. The eagle's wings are clipped; his soarings are never again to show the serene ecstasies of old. Yet what he can do, he still does majestically, and his renunciations give him command of a spiritual depth and intimacy which he has not touched before.

PLAN

The series of great songs that follow exhibits in various ways the new limitations under which the poet had to work. The idea of them was to develop more specifically than had been done earlier the spiritual and mystical side of man's experience. In theory they should have been a balance to the series that ended with the *Song of the Rolling Earth*, should have stood to it in the same relation as that in which *Calamus* stands to *Children of Adam*. They were to be the songs of that aspect of the mystery of life to which, as Whitman believed, death is the key. They were to proceed from that point of view, and to be the work of one "triumphant, disembodied, dead." The purpose was not wholly unfulfilled. Significantly enough, the first of them gives us a tossed and tossing paean in praise of music and the virtue of sound, "the soul's celestial dream," a poem full of intermittent splendour and bathos. The second, *Passage to India*, is more peculiarly representative; developing in these new contexts a theme treated already in *A Broadway Pageant*, it sings the love that would enfold the world and cannot rest until the world is enfolded and unified; until the soul, passing out beyond the world, in conscious aspiration embraces and claims all:—

> O Sun and Moon and all you stars! Sirius and Jupiter!
> Passage to you! . . .

Prayer of Columbus, which is next in order, is again unique. Written confessedly at a time of physical prostration, it all but sinks into a scheme of regular blank verse. But the theme, in its last seriousness, allows the poet no sacrifice of his characteristic exactitude and, in its individuality and perfection in weakness, the piece is a strange comment on Whitman's normal manner. We can scarcely measure the strength of the very strong except when it leaves them.

The Sleepers and *To Think of Time* are make-shifts. It is almost amusing to taste again in them the recklessness, the loose-woven textures of the expansive poet of '55. It is like bathing and buffeting the waves after having examined the fragile shells and faint patterns on the beach. Their position is easily explained; for the next section is to contain the first intimation of the approach of death. And yet how strange is their note of half-blended groping and positivism, and how irrelevant to the developing purpose of the book! The whole of the latter part of *Leaves of Grass*, we can scarcely assert it too often, exists only as a sketch. The framework—*Whispers of Heavenly Death, From*

Noon to Starry Night, Songs of Parting—indicates the trend of the idea ; but the outlines are filled in, for the most part, with irrelevant matter ; and the further we go, the more we feel how mistaken was Whitman's desire to give his poem an appearance of balancing parts. Still, we must beware of allowing too free a rein to our imaginative demands. If the sections with which we are now dealing disappoint us because of the incongruities they contain, we owe it to Whitman to take note of the associations of ideas which to his mind successfully overrode those incongruities.

Such a poem as *Chanting the Square Deific*, for instance, derives and was intended to derive weight from its position in the volume. It was written during the war, though with full power ; and it is easy to see why, if Whitman was anywhere to explain, as he does here, his theogony, he would wish to suggest that familiarity with death and acceptance of it were necessary to an inclusive conception of the Divine nature. *Whispers of Heavenly Death* aims, in fact, at representing the reflections of a man, whose powers are still at their height, upon the subject of his passage to the unseen. It was no part of the design of *Leaves of Grass* that failing power should appear in it (for that the annexes were reserved). The closing and completing experiences of life, with the larger and larger emergence of their unknown background, were to be treated, not indeed till life had yielded up and fully exhibited the contents of its treasure-house, but yet before the vital mechanism gave any symptoms of a decline. It was for this reason that the scheme of the book was blocked in, as we saw, so early; and only Whitman's peculiar, yet intelligible, insistence upon the war as the representative experience of his life necessitated the grouping of all about *Drum Taps*. Another idea now emerges. Before *Drum Taps* there were, particularly in *Sea Drift*, but also in an occasional hint casually dropped—in *Youth, Day, Old Age and Night*, for instance—anticipations of themes more proper to the concluding sections; similarly, in these concluding sections, reminiscent feelers are from time to time thrown back and the sense of the progress of life is combined with the sense of its underlying solidarity.

The title of the next group of poems *From Noon to Starry Night* enforces this idea; and the first piece in the group, clearly written as an introduction, shows that Whitman could not quite trust the idea to convey itself. *Autumn Rivulets* and *Whispers of Heavenly*

Death had also each their explanatory and artificial foreword; and in all this explaining we may trace in the poet's mind the dominance of conscious over unconscious motives. The formal and stylistic hesitancies of *As Consequent* and *Thou Orb Aloft* derive from the fluctuations of Whitman's purpose as he adopts the function now of the guide, now of the artist. In the same way *Thou Mother with Thy Equal Brood* is "placed" in a really atrocious introductory paragraph. The piece began originally with what is now its second stanza, its object being to depict the life of America —that is, of the typical democracy—as a summary of all that the past has bequeathed, the seed out of which the unknown future is to spring: that future which is to be greater, more resolute and more aspiring as the race continues to lay with increasing security the foundations of its self-knowledge.

To this world of towering possibilities, the individual, growing old, says his good-bye, his temporary good-bye. Such is the thought with which Whitman would bring us back to the main current in *From Noon to Starry Night.* The position of *Faces*, the first piece of the group, is a challenge. Perhaps its scorching candour connects it with the full glare of noon:—

This now is too lamentable a face for man,
Some abject louse asking leave to be, cringing for it,
Some milk-nosed maggot blessing what lets it wrig to its hole.

Yet the note of progress is dominant :—

The Lord advances and yet advances,
Always the shadow in front, always the reach'd hand bringing up the laggards . . .

and the poem closes, accidentally it would seem and yet appropriately, with a picture of old age. Whatever gave it its place, *Faces* has the finished, balanced, original, unpredictable periods of Whitman's best work, and his genius for word-impressionism is perhaps nowhere seen to better advantage ; nor, we must add, his early follies. The full-grown lily face that "speaks to the limber-hipp'd man near the garden pickets" reminds us of a confession made in late life that he would sooner cut off his right hand than write again some of his first passages. *O Magnet South*, *Mannahatta*, *Excelsior*, are early poems showing the same strong perfectness of form ; *The Mystic Trumpeter*, *To a Locomotive in Winter*, suggest failing power sustained by inspiring themes, while *A Riddle Song*, *What best I See in Thee* and *As I Walk these Broad Majestic Days* illustrate decline as well in conception as in execution. The ideal flavour of this group (a flavour suggested by its name and position rather than by anything very clearly traceable in its contents) comes out best perhaps in the short poem *By Broad Potomac's Shore.* *A Clear Midnight* reminds us of a vein of poetry missing in *Leaves of Grass,* though there are beautiful suggestions of it in *Night on the Prairies* and elsewhere. Certain passages in *Specimen Days* (particularly the meditation at the time of Carlyle's death) show that Whitman was qualified to relate human passion and experience to the emotional influences of the sky as fully as in *Sea Drift* he related them to those of the sea. Only from a hint or two dropped here and there or pieced together from that unpretentious, that almost lisping prose which is the most poetic creation of his later life, can we gather what the evocations of the *Starry Night* ought to have been.

In *Songs of Parting* we revert to a simpler general idea, though finding the same incompatibilities in the poems that realise it. *Years of the Modern* is not, as from its position we feel it should be, a poem composed in late life; it is placed here to suggest that what it expresses is what Whitman wished to express in the same breath as his farewell: the "more august dramas" of the future are still the focus of his attention. *So Long*, as we saw, and *Song at Sunset* also, are both early poems, the end of which they speak having been imaginatively foreseen. *Pensive on her Dead Gazing*, *Ashes of Soldiers*, and *Camps of Green* have all been brought forward from *Drum Taps*, of which they originally formed part, so as to emphasise the significance of the war in retrospect, and to express the fact that his experience in the war and the hospitals was to Whitman the gift and the illumination of his life :—

Give me exhaustless, make me a fountain,
That I exhale love from me wherever I go like a moist
    perennial dew,
For the ashes of all dead soldiers South or North.

Poetically, ideally, Whitman was after all right in making *Drum Taps* his centre-piece. He saw that the love that would be infused through materials must reject commerce with them except upon its own terms, and that the spiritual life, a continuous struggle for mastery, could recognise something analogous to itself even in the crude instruments of destruction. The soul builds with materials, but only that by their means it may build up itself ; and though its dependence upon them is more and more brought home to us as we see the material and spiritual welfare of mankind advancing collaterally, the last word is death, departure, independence, liberty. Liberty is the all-enclosing thought ; the soul that has once apprehended the conditions of liberty must acquiesce in the destruction of anything rather than that they should be destroyed. It is Whitman's triumph that, perceiving this, he mingles at once tenderly and remorselessly in his poems the thought of love and the thought of rebellion.

VII

CHILDREN OF ADAM

What do you seek so pensive and silent?
What do you need camerado?
Dear son do you think it is love?

Listen dear son—listen America, daughter or son,
It is a painful thing to love a man or woman to excess, and yet it satisfies, it is great,
But there is something else very great, it makes the whole coincide,
It, magnificent, beyond materials, with continuous hands sweeps and provides for all.

" DON'T you on the whole regret having written your poems of Sex?" the poet was asked by one of the many pilgrims who visited him in his old age at Camden. "Don't you on the whole regret that I am Walt Whitman?" was his rejoinder. *Children of Adam,* without a doubt, reveals his foundations to us, and to have withheld or withdrawn these poems would have been to abjure his calling. But the foundations have a twofold aspect. Internally what supports him is his intuitive conviction that every physical process has its spiritual significance, that the body is the counterpart of the soul. Externally, he has the buttress of his natural gift of self-assertiveness and antagonism. His aim, in *Leaves of Grass*, was not so much to make a statement of the truth in equipoise as to make a statement which, thrown in the scales against accredited views, would correct their bias and leave the balance adjusted accurately. He felt, for example, how much there was to be said on the side of conservatism, and would sometimes insist in conversation that he was a conservative himself. But he could trust the case for conservatism to get itself stated elsewhere; brute nature iterated it tirelessly; he therefore threw his whole weight upon the side of progress. His attitude to formal religion seems ridiculous or worse, until we recognise the same thought under it. Similarly in regard to sex. Nature's instincts of reticence had proved themselves, he thought, not only trustworthy, but too trustworthy. The demand of the future was for candour, not so much because candour was natural as because it was necessary: because without it there could not be the complete envisagement of this subject which was essential to an advancing civilisation.

The design of *Leaves of Grass* demanded from Whitman a cluster which should be devoted to the praise and solemnisation of sex. The source of his inspiration was a belief in the complete goodness of the universe; and the test of such a belief is, of course, its behaviour in the face of disturbing circumstances. What is more disturbing than the helplessness of our nature before the mechanical necessities imposed upon it by its association with the physical world? Man is a mere toy, liable to be crushed at any moment by blind forces; and in his sexual nature it often seems as if this blindness had taken its closest hold, exhibiting the material mechanism as part and parcel of himself, as a law imposed from within him. Such is the

> wearisome condition of humanity

which our own poets deplore, and such also was the thought of Sophocles, as we see in the stern rebuke he administered to that dullard who, in his old age, fondly enquired of him whether he was still a follower of Aphrodite, and learned that the poet considered himself as one freed at last from cruel masters.

But, human life on earth being, in Whitman's view, a phase only in the destiny of individuals, he holds that the human spirit attains through its apparent subjection to the physical world the differentiation, the identity which gives it its essential value. It becomes a "person," or, at least, enriches its personality. And if the spiritual life were really at the mercy of the material, if "matter were conqueror," his whole scheme would, of course, break down. The world is good because the soul is not in bondage, but has entered into a partnership with a reserve of ultimate independence :—

I but use you a minute, then I resign you, stallion,
Why do I need your paces when I myself out-gallop them ?
Even as I stand or sit passing faster than you.

To deprecate the material conditions of our life is thus, in Whitman's eyes, to miss the fundamental purpose for which we live. We are here to prove our souls, to refresh and to refine, to temper and to develop them by a continually widening experience ; and, such being his belief, he finds a corroboration of it in the mechanical arrangements which bring us here. The fact that nativity presupposes the fusion of two bodies may be regarded, if we please, as an accident of evolution ; it may be merely by a coincidence, too, that we describe the emotion that brings a father and a mother together by the name of love. But if the emotion in which the family originates is indeed the same as that in which religion finds the mirror of God, it is conceivable also that the very machinery of generation as it were epitomises the relation of the soul to created things. We are here in order to surrender ourselves to the world in an embrace and to realise ourselves through an inclusive union.

Sexual analogies are, of course, in a sense a commonplace of poetry. In all this, it might be argued, Whitman does not go beyond what every one who is capable of entering into a poet's mind allows. That is true; and yet there is a difference. The difference is that in poetry generally what we find is more or less illuminative allusion and comparison, whereas what Whitman offers he offers as a kind of germinal truth. The controlling influence of his life was his sense of a personal relation with the spirit that is interfused through all things, and like many to whom this sense has been present he could look back to a time in his life when it first illuminated him. Yet his description of this experience—

I mind how we lay such a transparent summer morning—

was one of the passages that the censor of morals wished him to withdraw. Again, though he theorises on this subject, he is never a mere theorist; his conviction coming to him from deeper, more visionary sources, theory and didactism overtake him only in certain applications and developments of a truth he has seen. Among his passages of purest poetry are those in which he celebrates the nuptials of the soul and the world :—

Smile O voluptuous cool-breath'd earth !
Earth of the slumbering and liquid trees !
Earth of departed sunset—earth of the mountains misty-topt ! . . .
Far-swooping elbow'd earth—rich apple-blossom'd earth !
Smile, for your lover comes.

Prodigal, you have given me love—therefore I to you give love !
O unspeakable passionate love.

The *Song of Myself* is built up out of this analogy, taking it, as we have seen, for a foundation and rising to it for a climax :—

There is that in me—I do not know what it is—but I know it is in me.

Wrench'd and sweaty—calm and cool then my body becomes,
I sleep—I sleep long.

I do not know it—it is without name—it is a word unsaid,
It is not in any dictionary, utterance, symbol.

Something it swings on more than the earth I swing on,
To it the creation is the friend whose embracing awakes me . . .

Do you see O my brothers and sisters ?
It is not chaos or death—it is form, union, plan—it is eternal life—it is Happiness.

If what Whitman here expresses is the truth he takes it to be, it is necessarily a two-edged truth; it devolves upon him to show in the experiences of sex themselves the quality in virtue of which they summarise the meaning of life. He only partially succeeded in this, but the attempt he makes is so noble that those who fully grasp and conquer his meaning will forgive errors by the way, and will probably come to recognise in *Children of Adam* an acceptable statement of a certain necessary stage of spiritual growth. The reader who grasps Whitman's intention without offence is, we must suspect, more civilised than the reader who is shocked by it. His idea might be put thus:—A man is not a complete man, nor a woman a complete woman, while they refuse to recognise, with all its implications, the faculty which made them and through them may make others. Very few are or can be at present complete in this sense; let that be recognised. But sooner or later the individual must rise to a perception of the sacredness of the fountain of life within him, and he will attain to this perception through trust, through a determination to find himself and be himself even in what may seem destructive or disintegrating impulses rather than in any inclination to distinguish himself from them and cast them off. It is in order to promote a sane self-realisation, to prevent the lurking of unacknowledged impulses in the dark corners of life, that Whitman writes *Children of Adam*, and in it relates,—as far as he can, exhaustively,—the psychology of sexual desire to the physiology of procreation.

A cardinal weakness which more or less affects all his utterances on this subject is that while his theories point inevitably to marriage as the consummation of the sexual life, he lacked the slowly accumulating experiences, disciplines, and revelations of which normal marriage is the vehicle and therefore celebrates as detached episodes events and impulses which imply a continuous relation. And this weakness is the greater, because we cannot feel it accidental to him that his life was a roving life. Whatever the circumstances that separated him from the mother of his children, the very fact that accepted severance did not preclude the arrival of a family is a certain indication of temperament. The catastrophe of his life had something in it that was appropriate to him. To this extent he must be called an " immoral " figure.

There is as it were a fabric of experience of which Whitman had grasped the plan, but which he had not in his own life built up ; and as a result of this, his attitude becomes in various ways misleading. It is expressive of his peculiar turn of mind that he attempts to represent sex as in a special sense a fusion of the past and future of mankind. He calls man in his sexual nature Adam, endeavouring to recover the simplicity and splendour of primitive relations, while yet it is clear that the relations he celebrates are to be realised in an ideal future to which humanity must grow. He seems here half enamoured of an illusion of which elsewhere he is free, the illusion of the "return to Nature." He connects the reticence of the civilised man and woman with "parlours," "delicatesse," and degeneration, and seems not to see its necessary connection with personal dignity. He writes that :—

> Without shame the man I like knows and avows the
> deliciousness of his sex,
> Without shame the woman I like knows and avows hers.

We may wonder in what circumstances or in what company such an avowal could be made —without doubt, a company of dismal theorists. Even if he meant only "acknowledges" "avows to himself" the note is still a false one; for shame is our equivalent for *pudeur*, and to attempt a dissociation of this feeling from the sexual impulse would be as it were to substitute the word " sire " for " father " or as if one should treat honour as accidental to the idea of a gentleman.

The eleventh section of the *Song of Myself* illustrates in an extreme form the confusions in which Whitman was involved. His aim in this passage is to extol the bare fact of sexual attraction. He puts before us the picture of a number of young men bathing, and watched without their knowledge by a young woman who desires to join them and in spirit does join them and gives her caresses to them all :—

> Which of the young men does she like the best ?
> Ah the homeliest of them is beautiful to her—

and so on. Whitman expected his readers to be shocked and disgusted by the candour of his description ; but he expected them slowly to recover from their shock and brace themselves to a manly recognition of truth. Yet his would-be simple picture turns out to be a tissue of follies and absurdities. His aim is realistic, but he has misrepresented feminine psychology. The young woman would not have cared to see the manly form, but to be seen by the manly eye ; her sex would not have driven her to be surreptitious in watching but to be conspicuous in avoiding the bathers.

Again, an animal left solitary becomes liable, no doubt, to undifferentiated desire, which the appearance of members of the other sex precipitates. But in the species man, this fundamental instinct is confronted with other instincts, less imperious perhaps, and yet not less authoritative—instincts responsive to the higher organisation of the life to which he has been raised and in which alone his sexual nature can unfold itself. These instincts call upon him to reserve his passion so that he may dedicate it to a partner of his choice. And this implies that the normal animal impulses, wholesome and inescapable as they are, cannot be, in human society, the themes for confident self-congratulation and rejoicing.

Whitman is to be honoured as a man who made great sacrifices for the sake of an ideal and was willing to incur distrust, contempt, and vilification. We do not detract from the honour due to him when we point out that his ideal was imperfect. One feature of it which is all strength is his insistence upon the equality in honour and mutual responsibility of the two parties to a sexual relation. As to the social conventions which have allowed differences of physical mechanism to become a means for the exploitation of one sex by the other, he does not deign to mention them.

His hymns of sex are hymns of the two sexes entering in reciprocal allegiance into a shared life. And this being so, he appears inevitably as a feminist. The woman's function predisposes her, of course, to a sheltered life; but civilisation, recognising this, has, sometimes under the name of chivalry, given her more shelter than she needs and produced at last in her a constitution barely adequate to the duties of maternity. The duty of a civilised community, Whitman holds, is to recognise the differentiations of sexual function with a view to redressing rather than intensifying the inequalities of opportunity to which they give rise. And one of his chief services to this cause is that he succeeds in bringing a real mutuality of feeling into his conception of the relations of the sexes. He is free from the false sentiment in men which sets up for worship an ideal of romantic ineffectuality. Yet he did not quite recognise that the demand he makes upon society to bring woman forward does not apply to woman in her sexual nature. It is as if he expected from the female the positiveness and even the initiative which are proper to the male, not seeing that a true development, while it will enable both sexes to understand one another, can never lead to any exchange or modification of fundamental impulses. With regard to this mutual understanding, the paramount duty is, of course, with men. For their own nature offers no problems to analysis, while the feminine instinct, with its attributes of envelopment and containedness, just because it is pervasive is evasive also; so that women who understand men so well understand themselves at present very imperfectly, while men have hardly made a start towards understanding them.

The chief disappointment of *Children of Adam* lies in its failure to express the central truth to which, one would have supposed, Whitman's whole philosophy of life was leading him. His governing perceptions in *Leaves of Grass* derive their light from two sources,—from his recognition of a pervading intersimilitude that binds all things together in one spiritual life, and from his recognition of the infinite and inexhaustible diversity of the self-poised, self-directing existences that breathe this common divine air. He is thus equally the poet of the universal and of the individual. But in treating of sex, while, as we have seen, his insight into its more mysterious implications, his presentment of it as the fountain of beauty and power, as Life undifferentiated and universal,—while all this belongs with what is most inspired in him, his attitude to it as a specific social problem suggests a mind removed and therefore fumbling. He still, it is true, speaks in clear, forcible terms, and draws on unfailing stores of righteous enthusiasm. But beyond saying that sex like all else is good, he gives little direction to his enthusiasm, and does nothing to show us under what conditions its implicit goodness will be realised. He seems indeed to make the fundamental mistake of supposing that the forms of truth as he has seen them in that upper transcendental air have only to be brought down and applied, like a transfer, to actual human life for all the conditions of what is right and beautiful to be fulfilled. In brief he sings not only sex the principle of life, but also sex the realisation, the source of lives, in the same universal language.

Yet this subject, more than all others, awaited and demanded the final differentiating word, the word which he is tireless in applying to literature, history, politics, however extreme the paradox in which the application seems to involve him :—

O I see flashing that this America is only you and me,
Its power, weapons, testimony are you and me,
Its endless gestations of new states are you and me . . .
Underneath all individuals,
The whole theory of the universe is directed unerringly to
 one single individual—namely to you.

Sex is celebrated, of course, as the origin or vehicle of the life of individuals :—

Underneath all nativity,
Underneath all the Expression of love for men and women.

But there is something more to be said and he does not say it. For surely if, as he believes and we believe, persons are the final unanalysable, concrete, everlasting fact; if the evolution of the world is a progress of personalities; if experience is the slow unfolding of personalities in the light they shed for one another and the light they share; if moreover it is of the essence of these personalities that each is individual and unique; where are we to look for the ultimate and specific meaning of a sexual relation but in the very fact of the uniqueness of the two selves who engage in it ? Its law, its mechanism, is universal, and a matter relatively insignificant. What is essential and inescapable is that two irreducible realities confront one another. It is not in the last resort an affair of organisms or impulses or gratifications; these aspects come and go and take a larger or a smaller proportion. Permeating all, the factor that always tells and cannot be eluded while the soul lives is that here souls, in their uniqueness, are present to one another, here souls interact : that from this union, since emotion is essential to it, they cannot be withdrawn. This truth never escapes the perception of the young lover while still, in the dawn of manhood, he retains the half-mystical instinct of his inexperience; and however far experience and disillusion pervert the mind, the truth still holds that it is not mere indulgence or dissipation that make vice vice, but, accompanying these things, the acceptance of the presence of another person to suffer or to share a wrong.

VIII

CALAMUS

O slender leaves . . . I permit you to tell in your own way of the heart that is under you . . .
I do not know whether many passing by will discover you or inhale your faint aroma but I believe a few will.

An air of mystery hangs about Whitman's *Calamus* poems ;—his poems of " adhesiveness " or the love of man for man. He advocates and to a certain extent himself practised an affectionate demonstrativeness which is uncongenial to the Anglo-Saxon temperament and which those Englishmen who forget that there are two sides to the Channel find even shocking. The result of this and of one or two expressions which occur in the poems is that he is quite generally suspected of a particularly unpleasant kind of abnormality. Addington Symonds, in his delightful monograph, throws the balance more heavily than was warranted in a direction along which other studies had led him, and hints that one purpose of *Calamus* was to provide a way of redemption for instincts of that kind. From what Horace Traubel tells us it would appear that he wrote to Whitman several times with questions about the meaning of *Calamus*, and the remarks in his *Study* show that even when he finally had Whitman's response he was not convinced by it. "I often say to myself about *Calamus*," Whitman remarks to Traubel —"perhaps it means more or less than what I thought myself; perhaps I don't know what it all means—perhaps never did know. My first instinct about all that Symonds writes is violently reactionary—is all for no, no, no. Then the thought intervenes that maybe I do not know all my own meaning."

In spite of Whitman's warnings that *Calamus* was not an attempt to reinstate Greek customs, Symonds develops the parallel between the ethic it displays and that of the martial Dorians at considerable length. But he only quotes one piece which really has any bearing on his analogy; and does not notice that even in *Earth, My Likeness* the final emphasis is laid upon reticence, fear even of avowal, by a poet who has fearlessly placed the whole of his character before us and acknowledged all the impulses, bad and good, of which he is cognisant in himself:—

Earth, my likeness,
Though you look so impassive, ample and spheric there,
I now suspect that is not all ;
I now suspect there is something fierce in you eligible
to burst forth,
For an athlete is enamour'd of me, and I of him,
But toward him there is something fierce and terrible in
me eligible to burst forth,
I dare not tell it in words, not even in these songs.

What then is the motive and justification of *Earth, My Likeness* if its meaning is not what Symonds supposes it to be ? In the first place, it includes what Symonds says is not included in *Calamus*, a recognition of an element of danger attending all highly-pitched personal emotion, the danger of an irruption of sex into a sphere in which it has no meaning. But in the second place, Whitman would not be content unless this dislocation of impulse, a dislocation after all so common, were acknowledged in his poems.

Not till the sun excludes you do I exclude you

is a thought which he would extend to those whose aberrations society finds unmentionable just as much as to those whose aberrations it perhaps mentions too glibly. This is, I believe, the only passage in *Leaves of Grass* that can be construed as an allusion to sodomy. Its meaning even so is not quite clear. But I interpret it as expressing recognition of an impulse capable of leading to that act, coupled with an assertion that the impulse, and obviously far more the act itself, is an unmentionable one. We have only to add that for Whitman there is nothing that can be done that cannot be mentioned.

Freed from the breath of this suspicion, *Calamus* appears as one of the most beautiful, if still as one of the strangest, of the subsidiary clusters of *Leaves of Grass.* In *Children of Adam* the functions of the body in that love into which bodily functions necessarily enter, were dealt with frankly; and the criticism put forward in the last chapter loses much of its force when we remember that *Children of Adam* is the praise of an abstraction, and that after it comes *Calamus* and fills in the blank spaces. "He does not celebrate love at all. It is as if the beasts spoke," wrote Thoreau in an early letter, and in the minds of most of his readers Whitman continues to stand as a man great, perhaps, but, unfortunately, shameless. Curiously, then, the note on which *Calamus* opens and which it maintains, is the note of shame, of *pudeur*. Sex, to Whitman's mind, is in all its operations as clear as daylight. Behind it the mysteries and the forces of life lie concealed; but its work in connection with those mysteries is transparent, and the difficulties connected with it come of the intensity and urgency of the instinct, difficulties only increased by dissimulation. *Children of Adam* is his protest against the suspicion that there is something shameworthy in the facts of the sexual nature in themselves. It is the praise of sex as distinguished from the praise of love, while *Calamus* is the praise of love as distinguished from the praise of sex.

Immediately in *Calamus* the sense of bashfulness, of reticence, which he cast aside so as to appear unaware of it, when he was dealing with physical desires and processes, comes over him with irresistible force. Why is this ? The sense of shame might be described as a refusal of the spirit to identify itself with and acknowledge itself in the material vehicle through which it works. We are ashamed when we feel that our actions do not properly represent us or do justice to us ; we are ashamed when appearances belie us or when we have allowed them to belie us or have been led away by them so as to belie ourselves. No more shame attaches inherently to the organs of sex than to any other bodily instrument. But to the emotion of love shame attaches peculiarly, because it is the endeavour to dedicate the entire self and because life provides no single vehicle for such a dedication. Love endeavours to imprint upon appearances meanings fuller, more comprehensive than they can bear; and thus it involves, in its very essence, an appeal to confidence and generosity, and the risk of misunderstanding and humiliation.

This seems to be the idea that underlies, or at least to be one of the ideas that underlie, that lovely and tantalising poem *Scented Herbage of My Breast*. Its aim is to associate together the ideas of love and death, to suggest that the true meaning of the relationship of souls transcends all the shows of life and is the fundamental purpose of the world. One of the chief difficulties is that the language, being throughout tentative and metaphorical, fits itself or seems to fit itself to the more obvious and more sentimental ideas which rising first in our minds oust Whitman's. The frequently quoted interrogation

(What indeed is finally beautiful except death and love?)

may seem to lend itself to a mood of pensiveness in which the mystical and the languorous merge. Whitman's mood is quite free from that taint:—

I will sound myself and comrades only, I will never again utter a call only their call,
I will raise with it immortal reverberations through the States, . . .

Through me shall the words be said to make death exhilarating,
Give me your tone therefore O death, that I may accord with it.

His point is that for the perfect emotion of love the condition to which he regards death as introductory is anticipated in this life, so that the whole material world and the body itself as a part of it are transcended and appear in their true light as instruments of spiritual progress :—

For how calm, how solemn it grows to ascend to the atmosphere of lovers,
Death or life I am then indifferent, my soul declines to prefer.

Calamus is thus the celebration of the ideal relationship of soul to soul ; and in order to divest this relationship of sexual associations, Whitman confines his hymns of it to the love of one man for another. But he does this by a poetic licence merely. It is equally of course the relation of woman to woman, or of man to woman in the rare cases in which difference of sex becomes irrelevant. Nor of course is it suspended in relations which are founded upon sex. It is suspended only when sex perverts or prevents a relationship.

The shame we feel in the voicing of this emotion Whitman connects with the fact that the expression of it, the interchange of it is a fundamental need. In loving and being loved the soul comes to knowledge of itself, and finds sustenance, a summons to action, the motive and the meaning of life. But only the soul loves, and the only object of love is another soul; and to know the soul of another is as difficult as to know one's own. Everywhere the dawning or developing impulse finds itself checked by barriers of appearance or thwarted by its own want of faith. Our shame when we love is our implicit knowledge that love is the only reality, rising up in rebuke of the explicit denials and shortcomings which daily life exhibits. The life of love is

> The life that does not exhibit itself, yet contains all the rest—

and when we love or ask for love, we as it were offer ourselves as embodiments of this all-containing life, so that our first thought is of our own unworthiness.

But the *Calamus* poems are mysterious in another relation, in relation to the personality of their author. Here let us first note that the 'I' of *Leaves of Grass* at the same time is and is not Whitman. It represents an identity detached from the confining accidents of existence, of which it can avail itself when it will, while yet when it will it transcends them. The 'I' has three stages. It begins as 'Walt' in his individual personal life. Next, it is that personal life regarded not as 'Walt's' merely, but as anybody's; the individual is made typical. Finally, it is the individual, and yet typical, life regarded not in its attainment but in its promise; it is the 'I' as it is revealed when everything accidental is parted aside and the enclosed seed of perfection, the soul of the soul, has been laid bare. But no distinction is observed in the poems between these three stages. They blend together, and the purpose of the book is to draw the reader imperceptibly from one to another, and so at last to reveal him to himself. Until he grasps this, the autobiographical directness of some of the poems puts him off his guard :—

What think you I take my pen in hand to record ?
The battle-ship, perfect-model'd, majestic, that I saw
    pass the offing to-day under full sail ?

and often as he reads the more mysterious confessions and declarations of the transcendental 'I' their drift is concealed from him.

Who is he that would become my follower ?
Who would sign himself a candidate for my affections ?
The way is suspicious, the result uncertain, perhaps
    destructive,
You would have to give up all else, I alone would expect
    to be your sole and exclusive standard . . .

This clearly is the 'I' which "waits" for each one of us within ourselves, that "bird of passage" which "through angers, losses, ambition, ignorance, ennui . . . picks its way." Different again is the 'I' of

These I singing in spring collect for lovers,
(For who but I should understand lovers and all their sorrow and joy ?);

for the actual and the ideal 'I' are interfused here, as we see in the continuation of the passage :—

Collecting I traverse the garden the world, but soon I pass the gates,
Now along the pond-side, now wading in a little, fearing not the wet.[1]

The beauty of it turns precisely upon its attribution to the ideal 'me' of actions which bring the casual, sauntering, musing Walt irre-

[1] Some readers may suspect the present writer of laying too much stress on supposed hidden or secondary meanings in *Calamus* and elsewhere ; others will quarrel with him for overlooking traces of a scheme of mystic symbolism. To his mind it is one of the symptoms of Whitman's power that, having in him so strong a bent towards mysticism, he recognised that the best expression of the "inexpressible" was to be found in terms of common speech and action. In the passage above and in some others he clearly uses a familiar image for its secondary suggestions. Briefly, "the garden, the world," is human life (cf. *Children of Adam*, p. 79), and the "passing of the gates" introduces us to the region of the beyond. It is in this beyond that we reach the pond-side where the poet wades in "fearing not the wet"; and it is here that we find growing, lifting its "tomb-leaves" out of the water, the Calamus-root which is Whitman's emblem of the love that is stronger than death. Readers interested in following out the more mystical side of Whitman's poetry and experience should consult Mr. Henry Bryan Binns's excellent *Life*.

sistibly before us; it is the mingling of the poetry that suggests a mood and the poetry that reveals an image. Whitman goes on:—

Alone I had thought, yet soon a troop gathers around me,
Some walk by my side and some behind, and some embrace my arms or neck,
They the spirits of dear friends dead or alive, thicker they come, a great crowd, and I in the middle,
Collecting, dispensing, singing, there I wander with them,
Plucking something for tokens, tossing toward whoever is near me,
Here, lilac, with a branch of pine, . . .
Here, some pinks and laurel leaves, and a handful of sage, . . .
But what I drew from the water by the pond-side, that I reserve,
I will give of it, but only to them that love as I myself am capable of loving.

What is this capacity? what is this ideal love? Every soul is, in Whitman's eyes, capable of it; and he only claims for himself capacity, not attainment. Indeed, *Calamus* bears out the impression which his history on the whole leaves with us, that he passed through life with the profounder personal longings of his heart unrealised. His relation to his mother, to his brother Jeff, to his young friend Pete Doyle, prove his natural gift for that interchange of details and trivialities on which the continuance of vitality in any friendship so much depends. But his life gives us no instance of a close and inclusive relation prolonged on equal terms and we are led to wonder whether he possessed the faculty which he most celebrates, the faculty of loving intercourse with equals. The question is one which a biographical psychologist might pursue almost endlessly; but the main fact to be held in view is that a man of his stature has little opportunity of intercourse with equals, and will probably meet none. Emerson was much older than Whitman; and even Emerson, much as he surpassed Whitman in intellect and in the range of his more sophisticated perception, had—who can doubt it?—a smaller store of that indescribable, undifferentiated power of beneficence and initiative, that central radiance, which is the final measurement of men. Lincoln was perhaps an equal; but even had the two men met, it does not follow because they were equals that they would have understood one another personally. We cannot bring Whitman to the test here; in regard to his private relations perhaps we can say no more than this, that he seems to handle them most perfectly in cases where the disparity between himself and his friend is most marked. From this it might be argued that he was not good at sustaining the appearances of equality when the conditions of sustainment were of the subtler kind; for in a broad sense, friendship, of course, equalises all. Yet it may also be, that the men more nearly capable of understanding him would be themselves lacking in the breadth, reserve and simplicity of nature required for comradeship with him. Whatever the explanation, Whitman's loss is the world's gain.

> I loved a certain person ardently and my love was not return'd,
> Yet out of that I have written these songs—

he confesses. And one of the most curious features of his work is that his claim to set up a personal relation with each one of his readers justifies itself. Thus he partly transcends that constantly bewildering dilemma which seems to present a choice to us between individual and universal love.

There is always the temptation to suppose that love as it becomes diffused becomes impersonal: that those to whom every man is a brother must take from their friends what they give to the world. Nor does the fact that an idealist like Shelley denies this affect us, if we seem to see in his own conduct an example of what he denies. Now Whitman insists always upon individuality, the relation to a person, as essential to love; the love which he extols as the most perfect is the love of friends who mutually single one another out and find spontaneous happiness in a unique spiritual affinity. Obviously no man can in this sense love everybody. Conversely, if a man is ignorant of such a love as this, can he, we might almost ask, love anybody? In theory, but not in theory alone, the reality of life to Whitman was individual men and women. He had faults of egotism and pride which even the splendid directness of self-expression attained in *Leaves of Grass* did not dispel. But he perfectly apprehended the difference between dreams and actualities in the sphere of the emotions; and when he speaks of the "ocean of love within him which he freely pours forth" we can analyse his words and reduce them to a series of loving actions, based upon loving perception of the differing natures of the men and women who crossed his path. The universal love of which he is a prophet does not reduce itself to a vague benevolence at the core of which we find the worm of comfortable self-deception. It is really the charity that begins at home:—

> In things best known to you finding the best, or as good as the best,
> In folks nearest to you finding the sweetest, strongest, lovingest, . . .
> Man in the first you see or touch, always in friend, brother, nighest neighbour—woman in mother, sister, wife—

Thus proved and substantiated, the power of translating love into action has its limits like all our other powers; yet it is the power which at the same time goes and takes us furthest, knitting us most widely and most variously with our fellows, and it is in this sense limitless that it transmits itself beyond the original occasion of its exercise and in its purer forms can, as it were, start waves of harmony which will vibrate through all minds that are attuned to them and so will encircle the world.

It is impossible to love everybody; but it is possible to feel so towards those with whom life actually brings us into contact that all who are touched by the reverberations of the feeling realise that they are virtually included in it. Perceiving this, and perhaps perceiving also that something in him went out more tenderly towards all he encountered than could ever be returned to him, Whitman conceived the idea of giving himself individually to all:—

> Whoever you are, now I place my hand upon you, that you be my poem,
> I whisper with my lips close to your ear,
> I have loved many women and men, but I love none better than you.

So it has come about that *Leaves of Grass*, for any one who cares to read it, contains this gift, all but unique in literature, of personal intimacy, a love that wakes response. Whitman's note of strong, undiscriminating tenderness has a Christlike beauty of appeal; his "neither do I condemn thee" (turn to *The City Dead-House*, reader) vibrates with a tumult of compassion; and when he admits the wistful insecurity of love, it draws us to him as nothing less human could do. He is the man

> Who knew too well the sick, sick dread lest the one he lov'd might secretly be indifferent to him,

he confides to us how

> When I hear of the brotherhood of lovers, how it was with them,
> How together through life, through dangers, odium, unchanging, long and long,
> Through youth and through middle and old age, how unfaltering, how affectionate and faithful they were,
> Then I am pensive—I hastily walk away fill'd with the bitterest envy.

He has, as it were, ripened and detached from himself a seed, which, wherever planted, grows to the image of the flower that bore it. It may be that we do not accept his methods of expression and in the picture we form of the man dislike some traits as much as we are moved by others ; yet in a region lifted above the conflicts of taste, we know that there has been brought to us a new ideal of the relationship of soul to soul ; and our hearts respond, feeling, with him, that here is the purpose of the world.

IX

DEMOCRACY AND THE INDIVIDUAL

She less guarded than ever, yet more guarded than ever . . .

Work on, age after age, nothing is to be lost,
When the materials are all prepared and ready, the architects
shall appear.

DEMOCRATIC government, the greatest experiment in which the human race has yet engaged, is still on its trial. In his trumpetings of its finality, Whitman lays open to the man of affairs what seems his most ingenuous side. Yet it would be a mistake to suppose him blind to dangers. If democracy is the "destin'd conqueror," there are

treacherous lip-smiles everywhere,
And death and infidelity at every step.

Indeed what makes his enthusiasm valuable is that while he avoids iterating what depresses and will always bring the positive aspect of things into prominence, he sufficiently indicates his perception of the urgency of the problem to convince us of his grit and candour :—

Forth from their masks, no matter what,
From the huge festering trunk, from craft and guile
    and tears . . .
Out of the bulk, the morbid and the shallow,
Out of the bad majority, the varied countless frauds of
    men and states, . . .
Health to emerge and joy, joy universal.

He has something of the sportsman's attitude in the face of evil, and can tolerate no mewling and whimpering over it ; to be matched against it, to stake all on overcoming it is the zest of the adventure of life :—

O to struggle against great odds, to meet enemies un-
    daunted !
To be entirely alone with them, to find how much one
    can stand !

The aim of his democracy is to make, in this sense, sportsmen of us all.

His belief in the possibility of it turns on his belief in the immortality of the soul. The belief is common ; yet, in the minds of most reflecting persons, we find it merging under pressure into one of the following substitutes. Some think that our immortality consists, not in survival of death, but in the fact that God always remembers the whole course of our lives ; others that it consists in the influence of our lives on history, the world bearing inscribed upon its rolls for ever the print of our transient activities; others that it is the faculty by which, while we live, we understand the nature of the things that never die—love and truth and beauty—and identify ourselves with them. These 'philosophic' substitutes would have seemed to Whitman merely evasive.

If all came but to ashes of dung,
If maggots and rats ended us, then Alarum! for we are betray'd,
Then indeed suspicion of death.

Do you suspect death? if I were to suspect death I should die now,
Do you think I could walk pleasantly and well-suited toward annihilation?

Pleasantly and well-suited I walk,
Whither I walk I cannot define, but I know it is good,
The whole universe indicates that it is good.

In a man of Whitman's complete freedom and sincerity of mind, who says what he thinks is true, not what he thinks it will be good for us to hear, this attitude is impressive. Moreover, though he is often a confused thinker, he is not often, one might perhaps say he is never, a confused feeler or a confused describer of his feelings; and his career was such as to submit this particular belief to the most searching of tests; he saw human lives poured out like water and in his own person knew the experience of death in life for a period of twenty years.

My hands, my limbs grow nerveless,
My brain feels rack'd, bewilder'd,
Let the old timbers part, I will not part,
I will cling fast to thee, O God, though the waves buffet
    me,
Thee, thee at least I know.

The basis on which he himself rests his belief is twofold. In his immediate communion with his fellow-men, with himself, with nature and the Spirit of all, he believed his experience to transcend the death of the body; he had the intuition of an immortal life. His reading of the concrete processes and development of events in society and history corroborated this; they were to his mind valueless, inexplicable, on any other hypothesis. The immortality of the soul was his first moral postulate. He uses it to give a new meaning to old formulas.

"Liberty, Equality, Fraternity," the watchword of Democracy, has been a motto much bandied about by revolutionaries whose chief aim was levelling and vengeance; and coming out of the mouths of unbelievers the words strike us with their inconsistency and with the blindness implied in them to obvious facts. We must sacrifice liberty if we are to equalise men, equality if we are to set them free. The spirit of fraternity suffers in either case. An equalised society would have to reckon with the resentment of men of naturally superior powers, and what is liberty if it means no more than the liberty to be fraternal? These objections do not apply to the motto as Whitman uses it. His love of liberty perseveres in spite of knowledge and avowal that its possession involves certain abuse. His doctrine of equality includes a recognition of all the facts of inequality; he even insists upon the necessity of them and upon the desirability of increasing them. He can preach the ideal of fraternity without cavil because he really has the fraternal temper.

Under the ideal of liberty he claims for each man the prerogative of his manhood; the right to have an initiative, an experience of his own; the right to develop will and character by using them; the right to know that his sufferings, his failures if necessary, are in part at least of his own making; the right to come into unmediated touch with circumstance and be a man among men, mixing in the clash and mêlée; the right to begin to be. To suffer life is not necessarily to be unhappy. Those to whom the course of their lives, with ways and means, is appointed from above may well, if the appointment is a fairly wise one, lead the most comfortable existences. The claim for liberty is not a claim for ease, but for conditions in which, pleasant or unpleasant, there is prospect of spiritual growth. The relation of the belief in immortality to this ideal lies in the weight of emphasis which is thrown upon the value of each individual's life when we believe that life to be susceptible of continuous development. If individuals merely partake temporarily of the stream of life, partly guiding, partly carried along by it while their brief hours run, the argument that each is severally of unique value, as representing something irreplaceable, something which has finally to be reckoned with in the scheme of things, breaks down. We may or may not believe that the wisest course for nations is to develop as large as possible a number of their citizens, the belief will be a matter for politics merely and the point at which individuals and generations of individuals can rightly be sacrificed for the preservation of the higher life of the few remains adjustable according to taste. But the belief in personal immortality, the belief that the individual soul is a centre of continuous and illimitable growth, necessitates refusal to accept the final subordination of one soul to another and cannot be content with any organisation of society in which such subordination is involved.

This leads us at once to the idea of equality. It is only in relation to an immortal life that the doctrine of the equality of men becomes intelligible. What appears often to be meant by those who say that men are equal is that the inequalities we now observe in them are due to the different circumstances by which different persons are surrounded, so that if the same opportunities could be given and preserved to all, an equality now only virtual would be actualised. This seems nonsense, and if individuality has in fact the value implied in the claims that Whitman makes for it, it would be a poor policy, even if it were a practicable one, to execute those claims in such a way as to damage the very cause we set out to advance. For what is individuality but differentiation? And what would be the use of supplying conditions and opportunities by common measure to persons to whom, *ex hypothesi*, the same conditions (even if the same could be supplied) would never seem the same?

The equality Whitman celebrates is subtler and more unseizable than this:—

> Do I contradict myself ?
> Very well then I contradict myself . . .

is his motto.

> Produce great persons, the rest follows

he says in one breath, and in another :—

> I only am he who places over you no master, owner, better, God, beyond what waits intrinsically in yourself.

The inclusion of the Deity in this list should satisfy the most exacting aristocrat. True, Whitman announces to all and sundry that

> There is no endowment in man or woman that is not tallied in you,
> There is no virtue, no beauty in man or woman, but as good is in you,

but, and here is always the underlying suggestion, this virtue, beauty, endowment, is a possibility, not an achievement ; it is what waits ; it is what is in you ; and the question is, when are you going to bring it out ?

> Have you outstript the rest ? Are you the President ?
> It is a trifle, they will more than arrive there every one, and still pass on.

The equality of men thus conceived is simply their immortality. Unequal as they are, it is intelligible to call them equal in this sense :—that the faculty of endless development which they share reduces their inequalities to a relative insignificance, since it removes them together immeasurably from the world of perishable appearances.

> Whoever you are! claim your own at any hazard!
> These shows of the East and West are tame compared to you,
> These immense meadows, these interminable rivers, you are immense and interminable as they.

Indifferent to the normal and familiar inequalities of life, this equality has nothing to fear and everything to gain from the spirit of freedom.

For to accept freedom is to forgo safety. It is to launch forth upon an uncharted voyage, to engage in an uncertain battle, ready to accept the lessons of defeat. And the importance of raising ever the cry of freedom, is that the nature of men acquiesces only too readily in conditions of servitude. Nothing is easier, nothing is more fatal, than to kow-tow. The superiority of one man to another makes itself so irresistibly felt that the knees of the lower type fail under him and he succumbs like one benighted in the snow. If we call "equality," it is to remind him of the goal he strives towards and which except by his own efforts he can never reach. Whitman's equality is thus a visionary equality, and his liberty, in our final understanding of it, the last achievement of the human spirit. The root of the matter is that life must be conducted so as to practise men from the beginning in the exercise of the qualities which lead them to their perfection. The luxury of stagnation must be refused to them, and into their lungs must be driven the keen air that brings pain and growth.

These being Whitman's ideas, we have to admit that they tempt him at times into strange places. He appeals direct to the individual and concentrates his whole force on producing in him a revived self-consciousness; he praises democracy because it has the same aim and sometimes forgets that it is the essence of democracy to be an aim rather than a fulfilment. Where, he asks in the *Song of the Broad Axe*, is the great city, and his answer runs :—

Where no monuments exist to heroes but in the common words and deeds, . . .
Where the men and women think lightly of the laws, . . .
Where the populace rise at once against the never-ending audacity of elected persons, . . .
Where the citizen is always the head and ideal, and President, Mayor, Governor and what not, are agents for pay.

The element of truth which these paradoxes are to drive home appears more plainly when he says :—

Where outside authority enters always after the precedence of inside authority.

His ideal is that each individual should be his own law, needing no external restraints and bowing down to no monument of others' virtue because he is himself virtue's embodiment. In a city where every citizen has justice thus inscribed within him, the functions of the officers of state will be merely formal, Whitman thinks; they will be like butlers and footmen, opening the door of the hall or the carriage when the master goes in and out. His point is that all the goodness available in the community at any time to sustain it is what is brought to it by its living citizens and enacted in their lives. Virtue cannot be imposed upon the state, but is inherent in it,—inherent, that is, in the individuals who compose it.

Here we touch the chief lacuna in his work. He has two ideals, the ideal of the growing man, and the ideal of the perfect state. The perfect state is a democracy, but it is a democracy, we seem to understand, because its citizens are perfect. If we ask Whitman how the perfect individuals are to consolidate themselves so as to work out and express their perfection in its communal form, his answer is, by fraternity,—they are to love one another.

Come, I will make the continent indissoluble,
I will make the most splendid race the sun ever shone
upon,

I will make divine magnetic lands,
With the love of comrades
The life-long love of comrades.

This is splendid, but unconvincing. Love is the motive power of unity, but before unity can be actualised, the power must be translated into a complex system of social activities. To put side by side, as Whitman does, the two words "individuality" and "en-masse" and to suppose that undifferentiated love will bridge the gulf between them is simplicity indeed. Or rather we might say that the word "en-masse" pictures well the confusion to which a number of loving and unorganised individuals must find themselves reduced.

No sane critic, we shall be told, would demand recognition from a poet of the mere machinery of life, how much less of the machinery of government! True enough; the poet soars high above these things; the world in which he is a native is a world in which they have been subsumed. But Whitman is, in this respect, not typical. For he is in a peculiar degree the poet of machinery. He delights to show how the advance of mankind postulates a developing material substructure. The building of a trans-continental railway or of a great canal, trade, the telegraph, the post, the press, these and all else that draws the minds of men into closer and more continuous communion, are, to his mind, great civilising influences. They are the condition of the attainment of human freedom. Bringing together the remotest parts of the world and making of the whole one organism, they are to inaugurate an enlarged humanity which will outgrow the figments, the routine-life of the past. The citizen of the future is to be a world-citizen; the amplitude of the earth, its "vast rondure," are to be repeated in him.

Thus Whitman cannot claim the poet's normal privileges. He who does not pretend to do more than choose, is welcome to make what choice he pleases. He who is for touching every note of the scale cannot complain if we remark on his omissions. In addition then to the obvious machinery of rods and wheels, to which Whitman does full justice, and to the less obvious machinery of flesh and blood, to which he sometimes does a little more than justice, there is the machinery of the documents, formalities and common customs which embody and preserve and give effect to the associated life and experience of communities and nations. These things cannot be superseded; least of all is it the idea of the true democrat that there can be any superseding of them. Whether or no perfect men could live without them is a theme for academic discussion. The strength of democracy is that it is not for the perfect but for the imperfect. For the difficulty here as everywhere is to secure a system which will not absorb the life for which it exists to provide a channel. Everywhere the flame of the present is menaced by the ashes of the past. Democracy is the ideal because it alone takes cognisance of the need for a continuous and automatic remodelling of its machinery with a view to the sloughing off of dead matter, appliances that have served their turn, customs that have become mere customs and so forth. With its incessant votings and canvassings, its suspicions and elucidations, its struggles, victories and defeats, its hopes and disappointments in which all according to their capacity have their share, democracy is the workshop in which the wheels are wrought over and the pattern brought up to date. Year by year it sends superannuated models to the scrap-heap and forges new weapons to meet new needs. And the zest of the enterprise comes of the perception that serviceable machinery is not to be had at any less cost and that the idea that proper arrangements once devised would settle our problems for ever is a delusion.

It was part of Whitman's mission, one would have supposed, to make these facts vivid. No one is more forcible than he in presenting, in other contexts, the principles they imply. What blinds him, perhaps, is the too facile distinction he draws between feudal Europe where liberty is an ideal to be contended for, and democratic America where it is attained. The result is that he forgets some of his own noblest announcements :—

> Now understand me well : it is provided in the essence of things that from any fruition of success no matter what shall come forth something to make a greater struggle necessary . . .

and allows himself to be ensnared into the belief that with the advent of the United States the essential is permanently secure. Yet the advent of liberty, rightly understood, is the advent of the perception that permanent security is impossible.

We were certainly entitled to expect *Leaves of Grass* to include the lovingest enumeration of all the functions and institutions, the muscles, bones, organs and viscera of the democratic body-politic. There should have been songs of parish councils and town councils, of voluntarily formed leagues, unions and societies, songs of presidents and chairmen, of treasurers and secretaries and committees and so on down to the mere voter or subscriber on the one side and up to the senator or cabinet minister on the other. The theme is forbidding, but other kinds of machinery have the same defect, and it did not frighten our Walt away from them. And the apparent dullness might have been an incentive; for all that is really necessary to life has the full value of the life to which it is necessary. Yet he turned a blind eye in this direction. Democracy to him meant certain spiritual conditions out of which he saw great individuals emanating. These individuals were so great, they were filled with so much spontaneous good feeling for one another and the world, that government became a dead letter, and for the effective voice of the nation and seal of its unity he looked not to its Parliament but to its literature. Criticism reached him, but did not penetrate :—

I hear it was charged against me that I sought to destroy institutions,
But really I am neither for nor against institutions,
(What indeed have I in common with them ? or what with the destruction of them ?)

With the destruction of them this :—and the remark applies as well to his conception of religion as to his conception of politics—that he announces times or conditions in which they will be outgrown :—

> Allons ! from all formules !
> From your formules, O bat-eyed and materialistic priests !

Such sweeping denunciation is not really a symptom of enfranchisement. The intellect, like the community, must indeed constantly test and revise its formulas; and the process is carried on, not because they are inessential, but because they are essential things. The aim is to bring them forward, to keep them level with the developing needs of thought. The danger of a formula is not that it is a formula, but that it may come to be regarded as something more. Thought is impossible without instruments of thought, life demands ordered and organised materials. But the instruments become obstructions, the materials cease to be organic and become parasitic, unless the mind ceaselessly remakes them, unless vitalising fluids tirelessly force their way through every shred of tissue. Formulas of some kind, institutions, the expression and preservation of communal experience, are as much a necessity to civilised life as machinery to locomotion. The spirit of liberty aims merely at keeping them in focus.

We cannot then wholly acquit Whitman of having, in a sense, sung the accidents rather than the essence of liberty. And even in his identification of the soul and the body, of the material and spiritual worlds, there is an analogous element of confusion. Room is left as it were for a residuary vagueness. He seems to suggest that materials, though they are the vehicles of experience, are treated best when they are treated casually. The opportunities which were presented to human effort by the size and wealth of the American continent are no doubt responsible for this airiness ; and yet, as a result of it, an essential point is missed. For our experience must remain vague and tentative till we can check it : till the conditions of our life bring the wheel full circle and enable us or oblige us to compare the credit and the debit sides of our account. So long as the life, whether of an individual or of a community, draws for its resources upon one blind margin and pours its waste into another, it has not attained its spiritual majority.

Yet his contribution here is not so much misleading as incomplete. He sees and expresses the truth in its general aspect :—

> No politics, song, religion, behavior, or what not, is of account . . .
> Unless it face the exactness, vitality, impartiality, rectitude of the earth . . .

He lifts us to heights from which the promised land is visible, and vitalises so much we took for dead that we are prepared for the perception, already dawning, that nothing is so. But on the whole it is rather the amplitude than the rectitude of the earth that he celebrates, and as well in regard to the economic as to the social machinery of life, he contents himself with a more or less unfruitful detachment :—

> I have loved the earth, sun, animals, I have despised riches,
> I have given alms to every one that ask'd, stood up for the stupid and crazy, and devoted my income and labor to others . . .

It is what we should have expected ; and yet it does not quite fulfil our expectations. It suggests rather the stock poetical attitude of aloofness, of protest against materialism, than the deeper vision which is always seeking for the exact valuation of material things.

Whitman's life afforded him practically no experience of the problem of poverty in the state, and gave him therefore no qualification for understanding the problem of surfeit. Yet it is an obvious corollary to the position he takes up, that the too-much or the too-little in a man's material equipment equally disqualifies him for the purposes for which we are all here—the knowing and adapting ourselves to things as they are, the experience and impersonation of truth. Perhaps there is consolation for the older countries of the world in the fact that, if they are penalised materially in having touched their boundaries and recognised the limits within which they must work, they are for that very reason qualified to draw better and more enduring nourishment from such resources as they have. For they are in a position to recognise, even if they are beaten by, the terms of the final problem. The liberty that depends upon our facilities for exploitation is an accident, not an attainment; it allows us to evade the laws of existence, instead of forming us by contact with them; it leaves us loose, it does not make us free. The test will come when all the wheels of the machine are brought into that final contact for which, if we are wise, we are preparing them. Then we shall know whether the cogs are designed rightly, whether they will run smoothly together or will grind and destroy the whole. Then it will be decided whether we have mastered our necessities and achieved freedom, or whether our civilisation is still but a spoilt child, and exists to the detriment of that long-suffering yet unforgetful world in which it is at large.

X

CONCLUSION: WHITMAN AND AMERICA

I am for those who walk abreast with the whole earth,
Who inaugurate one to inaugurate all.

Of all "adventures of a soul among masterpieces" *Leaves of Grass* affords, surely, the strangest. The climax of its strangeness is that it is deliberately strange; that strangeness has been achieved without the loss of mastery. Whitman challenged all the received forms, demanded a new form appropriate to a new ideal, and, in the very act of formulating his demand, fulfilled it. His work has a peculiar and an increasing significance. A prophet, he was without honour in his own country; but whereas as a rule it is the prophet's denunciations that alienate his people from him, in Whitman's case it was his complacencies. He epitomised his people so perfectly that he could make no impression upon them. To be in America so American was to be superfluous. His mission (as he himself recognised half wonderingly before the end) was to give America to the world. Writing for the mechanic, the pioneer, the rough, he forgot that the rough does not understand or care for roughness, craving perpetually to be smooth. His primary appeal is to those whose ear he would not have thought or cared to gain, to authors and teachers, to the cultured classes in this old feudal world, to those who are sophisticated and tired of sophistication, to those who are chafing against limitations they must abide by.

To his countrymen a vacuity, a proser, to Europe a refreshment and an antidote, Whitman bides his time and remains in equipoise, a figure to be assessed for his inherent value, apart from the natural actions and reactions which he excites. He is the poet of the principle of life, of the pilgrimage and progress of the soul, of perpetual effort and amelioration, of the joy of spiritual growth. Whoever we are, he will make a song of us and a song even of the imperfections on our heads. But if he sings what we have; it is for the sake of what we may and shall have; and so he reduces beauty and achieved goodness to the rank of camp-followers, banishing the dream of perfection by showing the reality to be at once inescapable and inapprehensible, bathing us always in the flow of an ever expanding fountain, pouring upon us always the waters of an ever rising tide. We can never tire of discovering him, for to discover him is to discover a new world, a new future, a new self.

In all this he is a representative American; representative too in that he stands, at first sight and perhaps finally, for the elevation of thought over form. In his own words :—

> The blood of the brawn beloved of time is unconstraint

or :—

> For the great Idea,
> That, O my brethren, that is the mission of poets.

This attitude, at once instinctive and deliberate with him, pervades his poetry and his life. Engrossed by the philosophy which gives everything to ideas, he yet had a natural philosophy of his own, and the recent developments of thought enable us to describe it; it was a kind of evolutionary vitalism. Art and beauty charmed him but they left him dissatisfied; and the cause of his dissatisfaction was that they seemed merely to summarise and rest contented with the past. Beauty, to Whitman, was the sign of the fulfilled; but the idea, the poet's mission, was the scheme and process of fulfilment, which continually ran ahead and anticipated the unfulfilled.

Whitman gave America to the world, and so constituted himself a national poet in a new sense. The national poet, singing the aspirations and the accomplishment of his people, sings them as a rule in such a tone and guise that they are recognised and acclaimed. It was the problem of American life to Whitman that she had produced no such poet. She had yet, he thought, to prove herself the compact nation, the unity he believed her to be, by giving birth to such a one. His loudest and most insistent demand was for an art which should be native to America, which should have the pride, the fierceness and the candour of the only emancipated people of the world. It disappointed him to find that his own muse was rejected. He believed in the advent of a new race of poets, but he believed himself to be at least their harbinger. How was it that the America, to whom he owed and to whom he had given all, failed to recognise herself in him? He was baffled and he had the right to be so. The key to the mystery gives us the significance of his peculiar place in literature.

It is so much a commonplace of criticism that great art is produced at periods of intense national activity and enthusiasm that the connection between the two has passed almost into a superstition. We think of the artist as a rule as a man who has been endowed with an abnormal capacity for feeling; yet the essential distinction between the artist and other men is not that he feels more than they do, but that he has a native impulse to the expression of his feeling, to the expression of it in a particular kind of way. Art has two aspects: if on the one side it is pure spontaneousness, it is hedged on the other with dexterities and technicalities. The artist is a man so practised in accomplishment that what to others would be artifice is to him spontaneous impulse; and the difficulties of expression are so severe that accomplishment of this kind involves inherited faculties adapted to inherited conditions of life. The individual does not attack the problem of expression in its elements; he merely advances by a stage the solution of it to which the manners and customs of their country, the intellectual and spiritual atmosphere of their age, have conducted his predecessors in the field.

Yet, if the impulse and faculty of expression is the artist's peculiar attribute, the first condition of artistic expression is the existence of the feelings which are to be expressed. The artist must have supreme mastery over his material vehicle, he must also have an abounding rapture, to maintain his assurance of a message. The craft, itself so slowly perfected, appears now as a system of hindrances which the art must overcome; and here again the artist remaining single-handed remains powerless. His exultation, if it is to triumph, must be fostered. The logs which blaze merrily when we bring them together lose their heat when they are divided, and the glow from which the light and flame of poetry rise is more than a man can generate or maintain in isolation. If he is to give himself wholeheartedly to expression, what he expresses must, as it were, be matter of course. It must be not his own but everybody's feeling. It must be the thought that finds expression through one because expression is demanded for it by all.

In other words before a national poet can arise, the way must have been prepared for him. The temper of his people must have put on settled and salient characteristics which he can translate. Poetry, if it is to appear in miniature as a form of words, must first have been incorporated on a majestic scale by the community. It is the expression on the face of life; and a nation, before it can have a poetry of its own, must possess and include the qualities which that poetry is to show forth. From experience grow ideas and from ideas aspiration.

In America the process had been inverted. The spirit had anticipated the people. Aspiration and ideas existed ready-made and were engaged in finding experience and establishing themselves. The flower and fruit of a civilisation had been borrowed; the vital movement of the people was towards the formation of roots and branches. Conditions were wanting, therefore, for the rise of a school of native craftsmen; and Whitman, though he did not reckon with all the implications of this fact, seized upon the essence of it intuitively. He saw that there was no American tradition in poetry, and that the English tradition, if only because of its consanguinity, must be worse than useless to him. He was prepared to dispense with what he could not have. No peculiarly American form, manner or associations had been elaborated; he must forgo the thought of such a thing. But from the sacrifice he would draw an advantage. His country had given him no literary instrument; his want of an instrument should be his escape from the tricks and trials of the instrumentalist. It was of the essence of the American spirit to assert that set forms were inessential; in him they should become so. He would launch forth upon a career of spontaneous and unfettered self-expression. His instrument should be himself.

Thus he turned his chief deprivation into a source of power. The typically American civilisation was in the womb of time. His country, therefore, before his devoted eyes, merged into the type of an ideal future. Democracy and America are interchangeable words in his vocabulary and it is the virtue of America that she is democratic, not of democracy that it is American. He preaches fervently the doctrine of the unity of the whole people; that the doctrine needed preaching is significant of his position. America, he believed, was to achieve nationality and to transcend it. The inspiration of his work, perhaps for the first time in literature, is a hope which leaves nationality behind, a hope unrealisable until the nations look beyond themselves and become limbs in the body of a united race :—

> O America because you build for mankind I build for you.

Nevertheless, he made it deliberately his business to " tally " the land, the people, as they were; he laid himself open to all the impulses which were astir in them, to all the persistent and subtle influences of scenery, soil, climate, occupations. His task completed, he expected recognition. Yet recognition did not and could not come. For self-consciousness implies maturity ; incompleteness cannot recognise itself. With infallible sincerity and intuition Whitman had held up the mirror of art before an unformed race and had given to it for its delectation the word 'growth.' Growth is not a delectable word to those whose task it is to be growing. There is even a flavour of tactlessness in the use of it under such circumstances. The idea of growth, the growth of the spirit, does not present itself to normal minds until the material preparations for it have been completed. In the mind of the poet a vicarious completion takes place. The material incompleteness of his environment ceases to be a hindrance to him when he sees in it a direct relation to the formative principle within him. He takes it as a type of the condition of spiritual progress, and finds in it the essence of the meaning of life.

It was natural then that America should refuse Walt Whitman. He could not give her what she wanted ; for he could only give her what she had already given him. She gave him her aspirations, universal, untried ; she gave him her opulence, her variety, her vast spaciousness, her wild margins evoking enterprise. The counterpoise, the balance of the two, she could not give, because she had not effected it. America's accomplishment it will be for the future to reveal. Poets, if that accomplishment proceeds organically from the conscious life of a nation, will draw fire from it and find new forms for its expression. They will reflect a national achievement, and the nation will recognise in them the reflection of what it has achieved. In the meantime her contribution to the world has been and is the infection of her undaunted youth. The world as it grows old keeps learning and keeps forgetting the meaning of what it has learned. A new start in a new world brings out the first lessons of things, their larger outlines, with reviving clearness. America stands for the passionate reassertion of certain beliefs which life, to those who look back upon it, seems always to stultify, but which, to those who can look forward, appears as the very spirit and power of life itself—" the urge, the ardour, the unconquerable will." With these the spirit of Whitman was impregnated; and, burning with the determination to express them, he cast aside everything that seemed to choke and imprison him, counting the great traditions of poetry worthless in comparison to them, staking all on his intuitive knowledge of poetry as a living presence in himself. The work of the culminating poet is to celebrate conquests achieved, to express an established civilisation; and his fellows acclaim him, because he does but build again in a new material what they, in the common materials of life, have built already. Whitman was poet not of the achieved but of the achieving. "Man never is, but always to be blest"; say rather, it is his blessing to become himself, an infinite process. The conditions of life in America in Whitman's time were such as to change a commonplace into a source of inspiration. Seeing everywhere the scaffoldings of life thrown up, he too threw up his scaffolding and proclaimed the eternal significance of rope and pole. He rises thus above nationality and becomes a universal figure: poet of the ever-beckoning future, the ever expanding, ever insatiable spirit of man:—

O give me the clew! (it lurks in the night here somewhere,)
O if I am to have so much, let me have more!

THE END